Fix Your Broken Windows

*A 12-step system for promoting
ethical affluence*

Yonason Goldson

New revised edition

Timewise Press
St. Louis, Missouri

[handwritten inscription: Thank you, Mike, for joining us @ NSA STL]

Fix Your Broken Windows

Yonason Goldson

FIX YOUR BROKEN WINDOWS

Timewise Press
St. Louis, Missouri

ISBN: 978-1981837557

Please send all correspondence to:
info@ethicalimperatives.com

Cover image © Can Stock Photo / infinity3d

For Rabbi Gabriel Munk

a prince among principals
a hero among headmasters
an angel among administrators

TABLE OF CONTENTS

PREFACE TO THE NEW EDITION

When I first published *Fix Your Broken Windows* two years ago, it was little more than an anthology of published essays, freshened up and arranged to provide a collection of insights for how little changes in behavior foster personal success and professional affluence. It was merely intended as a companion to my keynote programs that would further stimulate thought and promote a mindset of ethics.

Since then, I experienced two revelations.

First, I was approached by a friend and neighbor who asked me to design a program for fostering collaborative spirit among his employees. He intrigued me by proposing that I model the program according to the teachings of one of Jewish tradition's most influential leaders and thinkers.

In 19th century Europe, the revered sage Rabbi Israel Salanter created what has become known as the *mussar* movement, a philosophy of personal improvement through character refinement and self-awareness – what today might be called mindfulness. As an outline, Rabbi Israel assembled a list of 13 character traits that form the essence of a fully functional, ethically responsible human being.

In a flash, I envisioned an alignment of his 13 traits with the 12 sections of my book.

After a long incubation period, inspiration struck a second time. It occurred to me that I could provide a more effective guide by structuring my own 12 steps according to the classic 12-step recovery programs that had inspired the title to begin with.

Why are recovery programs an appropriate model for an ethics program? Because the truth is this: *we are all addicts*.

And what are we addicted to? The status quo.

We talk about change, protest for change, vote for change. But we really don't like it very much. We talk about the need to get out of our comfort zones, but we resist taking action to do so. After all, it's uncomfortable.

That's why the road from dysfunction to sound physical and mental health requires a system. That's why 12-step programs work.

If they work in our personal lives, why shouldn't they also work in our professional lives? If a system can wean us off chemical addiction, why can't it prod us into more ethical behavior as well?

With that in mind, I have adapted the 12 steps into a new ethical context, matched them up with the character traits advanced by Rabbi Israel Salanter, and reorganized the chapters of my book to fit into the new model.

The result, I hope, is a more systematic approach that provides not merely insights and inspiration by an actual roadmap that leads to recovery – recovery of civility and respect, of trust and loyalty, of empowerment and enthusiasm, of passion and productivity.

The road lies before us. Let's walk it together.

THE 13 TRAITS OF PERFECT CHARACTER

HUMILITY
Rather than fixating on what the world owes us, we should ask what we are contributing to make the world a better place

PEACE OF MIND
We flourish when our mood is calm like a lake, not churning like the sea

ENTHUSIASM
Every moment of life is a priceless opportunity

TRUTHFULNESS
Our words must be true, but also our thoughts, our actions, our intentions, and our aspirations

ORDER
Setting priorities keeps us focused and efficient

DILIGENCE
Anything worth doing is worth doing to the best of our ability

SILENCE
We learn only through listening; the same letters that form *listen* also form *silent*

RESPECT
Every person is entitled to be treated with dignity

JUSTICE
When we value fairness, we encourage others to do the same

CLEANLINESS
Good personal hygiene makes for a healthy body; psychological good health comes from good habits and attitudes

PATIENCE
Success, like growth, cannot be rushed or hurried

PLEASANTNESS
Engage every person with a pleasant demeanor and speak all your words softly

THRIFT
Resources are limited; take what you need, and be happy with what you have

THE 12 STEPS TO ETHICAL RECOVERY

1. Admit that you have no control
2. Acknowledge a power greater than yourself
3. Commit yourself to a higher purpose
4. Articulate your errors
5. Make a searching and fearless moral inventory
6. Look beyond yourself and enact all necessary steps to improve your character
7. Listen to understand the ideas expressed by others
8. Articulate back to others their ideas so they know they have been heard
9. Recognize personal bias, emotion, and irrationality
10. Reject double standards and intellectual inconsistency
11. Through self-reflection and meditation, seek deeper awareness of purpose, knowledge of truth, and the wisdom to implement them in your life
12. Be a model that inspires others

INTRODUCTION

The Cost of Disrepair

In 1982, George Kelling and James Q. Wilson published their soon-to-be-famous article "Broken Windows" in *The Atlantic*. The premise was simple. Small signs of neglect snowball into chronic and systemic decay.

That principle became the cornerstone of Rudy Giuliani's anti-crime platform as mayor of New York City. Police adopted an aggressive approach toward loitering, panhandling, littering, graffiti, and fare-beating – to name a few. They also began their now-infamous stop-and-frisk policy. The city rapidly became one of the safest in America, and everyone celebrated success in the war on crime.

However, as time passed, some began to question whether "broken windows" really deserved credit for New York's turnaround. Yet George Kelling continues to defend the soundness of his theory, arguing that over-reliance on law enforcement fueled community resentment that gradually undermined the program:

> *"Good broken windows policing seeks partners to address it: social workers, city code enforcers, business district improvement staff, teachers, medical personnel, clergy, and others. The goal is to reduce the level of disorder in public spaces so that citizens feel safe, are able to use them, and businesses thrive."*

Let's leave the debate about New York City to sociologists and politicians. In terms of human psychology, the principle is solid. We all respond to subtle cues, be they visual, aural, or emotional. Often, we aren't conscious of our own reactions, or of what's causing them.

Just as a coworker's humming or pencil-tapping drives us mad, other nuances of our environment have a corrosive effect upon our attitudes, even if those nuances are not profoundly negative themselves. These are the "broken windows" that can create a tense – or toxic – workplace.

Just how bad is it? According to estimates, lost productivity in the United States each year from employee disengagement adds up to between 450 and 550 *billon* dollars.[1] And an estimated $359 billion is lost each year due to workplace conflict.[2]

But just imagine! If little vexations can disrupt our mood and our efficiency, isn't it likely that little positive changes can similarly enhance and improve our outlook and our productivity?

Fixing a few broken windows can produce dramatic results. And it's not even a new idea. Nearly 3000 years ago, King Solomon said, *One who leaves a hole in his fence invites in a snake.*

A little neglect can prove costly, even fatal. So don't wait for disaster. Start fixing your windows now and see how many other problems start fixing themselves.

As George Kelling explains, success requires group participation, effort, and cooperation. Inspired by his model, I offer the following 12-step process of simple changes for any culture to improve its ethical health and thereby achieve increased affluence.

---

[1] Gallup estimate, 2012
[2] CCP Global Human Capital estimate, 2008

CHAPTER 1

Behind Window Number 1

Make Better Choices

Have you ever stood in the supermarket aisle debating whether this brand was better than that brand, whether the big box was worth the savings-per-ounce over the small box, whether it was worth the risk to choose an unknown product that you might love or might hate over sticking with a brand that you know that you like?

Did that make you happier?

Malcolm Gladwell seems to think so. In his 2004 Ted Talk, he recounts the career of one Howard Moskowitz, a psychophysicist whose market research for Pepsi Cola, Vlasic Pickles, and Prego Spaghetti Sauce – beginning back in the early 70s – changed the food industry forever. It might seem obvious with the wisdom of hindsight but, to make a long story short, Howard Moskowitz discovered that there is no perfect pickle, no ideal type of cola, and no universal favorite recipe for spaghetti sauce.

As a result, we ended up with seven different kinds of vinegar, and 14 different types of mustard, 36 varieties of Ragu spaghetti sauce, and 71 variations of olive oil. As options increase, prices go up. And Mr. Gladwell tells us it's all worth it:

That is the final, and I think most beautiful lesson, of Howard Moskowitz: that in embracing the diversity of human beings, we will find a surer way to true happiness.

But we might want to ask ourselves this: When Thomas Jefferson famously articulated our inalienable right to the pursuit of happiness, was he talking about our choice of mustard? Is a perfectly brewed cup of coffee the ultimate means of becoming, in Mr. Gladwell's words, "deliriously happy"? Is paying a premium for the ideal condiment symptomatic of a perfectly content and psychologically healthy society?

Science suggests otherwise. In her own 2010 Ted Talk, psycho-economist Sheena Iyengar describes how surprised she was to discover that recent immigrants from former communist countries did not see a choice between seven kinds of soda as a choice at all; rather, they saw one single choice: *soda.*

Here we find a compelling example of life imitating art. Do you remember the scene in *Moscow on the Hudson* when Robin Williams breaks down in the supermarket aisle because he wants to buy coffee and can't cope with the endless, indistinguishable choices available to him?

So who is better off? The person who has many choices, or the person who *doesn't see a need to choose?*

Dr. Iyengar explains it this way:

When someone can't see how one choice is unlike another, or when there are too many choices to compare and contrast, the process of choosing can be confusing and frustrating. Instead of making better choices, we become overwhelmed by choice, sometimes even afraid of it. Choice no longer offers opportunities, but imposes constraints. It's not a marker of liberation, but of suffocation by meaningless minutiae. In other words, choice can develop into the very opposite of everything it represents...

She goes on to suggest that we reconsider three basic assumptions about choice:

- It is always good to make your own choices.
- More options lead to better choices.
- You must never say *no* to choice.

If we are choosing between irrelevancies, if we are overwhelmed with options, or if we don't have enough information to choose wisely, does it make any sense at all to conclude that we're better off just because we have the right and the opportunity to choose?

Dr. Iyengar adds:

A number of my studies have shown that when you give people ten or more options when they're making a choice, they make poorer decisions, whether it be health care, investment, or other critical areas. Yet still, many of us believe that we should make all our own choices and seek out even more of them.

Experience indicates that just the opposite is true. When we have more choices, we also have higher expectations of getting exactly what we want, a lower tolerance for imperfection, and a more persistent feeling that we've missed out on something better.

Dr. Iyengar offers a case study of women given a choice between two shades of pink nail polish. Half of them thought they were being tricked – that both shades were actually the same – and the other half chose names over hues, preferring "Ballet Slipper" pink to "Adorable" regardless of the actual color.

So are we all condemned to remain victims of too many meaningless choices, or is there something we can do about it? And how much productivity is lost because we quibble or agonize over trivial choices rather than applying our attention to substantive decision-making?

Let's start by translating Dr. Iyengar's challenged assumptions into action. By doing so, we can arm ourselves with a list of criteria to check off whenever a legion of choices comes storming over the horizon.

1. **Am I buying into a false comparison?** Professor Dan Gilbert points out that the same people who would pay $1600 for a Hawaiian vacation discounted from $2000 would pass on the same vacation for $1500 if they had just missed a special that offered it for $1000. In other words, "a good deal that was once a great deal is not nearly so attractive as an awful deal that was once a horrible deal." Look at the choice itself, not the choices all around it.

2. **What if I don't choose at all?** Is there someone more qualified, more objective, or more informed to make the choice? And maybe the choice is really a distinction without a difference: if no choice gets made at all, will anyone notice or care?

3. **Am I overwhelmed with options?** Brainstorming works up to a point. But when too many choices start to blur together, an overloaded mind almost guarantees choosing poorly. Start with a process of elimination by

weeding out the worst alternatives first. If you can get down to a manageable number, then you can think about deciding. If not, sleep on it.

4. **Am I being impatient?** Again, Professor Gilbert points to research that most people will choose $50 now over $60 a month from now, but choose $60 in 13 months over $50 in 12 months. If we can wait later, we should be able to wait now. But immediate gratification distorts our reasoning.

5. **Am I thinking rationally?** Emotions play a disproportionate role our decision-making. When you feel your hormones, your endorphins, or your impulse for immediate gratification kicking in, it's time for a time out. If all else fails, call a friend whom you've prepped to act as your rational anchor. Alternatively, carry a pair of handcuffs at all times so you can lock yourself to the nearest parking meter.

6. **Do I have enough information to choose wisely?** When it comes to big decisions, like college, marriage, and presidential elections, do you know what you're committing yourself to? This may be a corollary of Number 5, since a flood of emotions easily blinds us to our own ignorance as well as our own impetuosity. Choosing out of ignorance is a synonym for stupidity.

King Solomon says, *Wise choices will watch over you, and discernment will guard you.* A healthy dose of reality always makes for the best possible choice – even if that means making fewer choices from fewer options. In the end, we will likely discover that by choosing less we will end up with more time, more peace of mind and, yes, more happiness.

One more thing: be careful not to let yourself be swayed by those who insist, like Starbucks, that "Happiness is in your choices."

That's their choice. As for me – I take my coffee black.

Practical Applications – *Dos* and *Don'ts*

- Do look for happiness in the quality of your choices.
- Don't look for happiness in the quantity of your choices.

- Do consider whether or not a choice provides genuinely different options.
- Don't overvalue choice for the sake of choice.

- Do make the effort to fully understand the choices before you.
- Don't be seduced by false comparisons.

- Do take your time before making important choices.
- Don't be bullied into making choices you aren't prepared to make.

- Do relinquish the right to choose when choosing does not serve you well.
- Don't presume that a choice matters when you can't find a good reason why it does.

Step #1: Admit that you have no control
Trait #1: Humility

Too many choices can be as paralyzing as no choices at all. If so, how many is the right amount of choices?

It doesn't matter.

Why not? Because we have no control over the choices we *have*; all we control is the choices we *make*.

Even then, we control only our decisions, but not where those decisions will lead. History is filled with stories of sure things that went down in flames and errors that led to spectacular success.

This does not mean abdicating responsibility. As Dwight D. Eisenhower said: *Plans are worthless, but planning is everything.*

Humility doesn't mean denying your talents or devaluing your contributions. It means reframing success as a gift and a duty to the world instead of a prize to won at others' expense.

You may not have Michael Jordan's ability on the court or Steve Jobs's genius for innovation. You may not have Scarlett Johansson's good looks or Sara Blakely's business acumen. But you do have the potential to play the cards you're dealt the best you can, to make the most of your unique circumstances, to respond to the choices that appear before you with thoughtful determination rather than react to them out of frightened desperation.

Most of our anxiety comes from thinking we have control when we don't. Recognizing what is and is not in our hands empowers us to act rationally and decisively while leaving the outcome of our decisions in the capable hands of providence.

CHAPTER 2

The Emperor's new Windows

The better you look, the better you'll be

Take a ride in a glass elevator, from ground level to rooftop in a single ride. How do you feel?

If you're like most people, you feel – no surprise here – like you're on top of the world. You feel good about yourself and believe in your ability to overcome any obstacle and conquer every challenge. The only downside is – well, going down. By the time you get to the bottom, not only have your feelings of grandeur evaporated, but now you feel a bit puny, somewhat insignificant, and less than capable.

But wait! You can save yourself the effort. Researchers have discovered that you can awaken the same responses by merely *imagining* yourself soaring skyward or plummeting earthward. With a little visualization, you can create your own mood.

But what happens next?

That's what Max Ostinelli, David Luna, and Torsten Ringbergat wanted to find out. The three psychologists at the University of Wisconsin, Milwaukee, asked subjects to imagine themselves rising up into the sky, then asked them to solve a series of SAT-style math problems. With all that positive self-esteem pumping up their neural pathways, certainly their performance should have increased significantly. Right?

Wrong. They did worse. A lot worse. In fact the performance gap between those who had their self-esteem artificially inflated and those who had theirs artificially diminished was between 20 and 30 percent.

As Max Ostinelli explained to NPR, "When we boost self-esteem in this way, people are motivated to maintain their self-esteem. So they say, well, I'll withdraw from the task."

In other words, when we know that our feelings of accomplishment are unearned or undeserved, our defense mechanism kicks in to protect our fragile bubble of fantasy from the nasty pinprick of reality. Conversely, when we feel we have to prove ourselves, an inner voice prompts us to engage and persevere rather than sit around wallowing in our feelings of inadequacy.

The research team repeated the experiment with a different task, this time shopping for a cell phone plan. And once again, the people who felt good about themselves put less effort into their research and chose poorer plans, while the subjects who needed to restore their self-image investigated more carefully and found better deals.

It's a bit disconcerting that we actually have so much control over our own self-image and, consequently, our own level of achievement. What other subtle cues might we send ourselves to improve our performance?

What about the clothes we wear? Is it logical to assume that dressing up will produce negative results similar to the imaginary elevator ride upwards, and that dressing down will yield positive returns like the imaginary elevator ride down? Is casual attire a beneficial stratagem to workplace productivity?

Probably not. And here's why:

Why do we say *dress for success?* Because we know we have some standard to live up to, whether it's a date, a job interview, or a sales pitch. By putting thought and care into our appearance, we remind ourselves that we have to take the situation seriously if we want to be taken seriously. On the other hand, if we dress like we're headed out to the backyard for a barbeque, our mindset is likely to define our demeanor.

Dr. Karen Pine, Psychology Professor at the University of Hertfordshire, explains it this way:

> "A lot of clothing has symbolic meaning for us, whether it's 'professional work attire' or 'relaxing weekend wear,' so when we put it on we prime the brain to behave in ways consistent with that meaning. This theory supports the notion that we would stay more focused when wearing work clothes, and may be more cognitively alert than if we dressed down."

Of course, there are exceptions. But most companies are not Facebook or Google and shouldn't expect to operate as they do. This doesn't mean everyone needs to wear a suit and tie. But it does suggest that a professional-looking work environment promotes the mindset of professional standards and achievement.

So save the blue jeans and the cargo pants for the weekend. If you look like a million bucks, you may be on your way to closing that million-dollar deal.

And don't think too highly of yourself before you've earned the right to do so.

Practical Applications – *Dos* and *Don'ts*

- Do set goals for yourself.
- Don't imagine that you've already attained them.

- Do visualize yourself achieving your goals.
- Don't visualize that you've already achieved them.

- Do challenge yourself to perform better.
- Don't allow yourself to believe that you're doing as well as you could be.

- Do present yourself in a way that holds you to a higher level of personal conduct.
- Don't be casual except when it's time to relax and unwind.

- Do associate with people who value professionalism.
- Don't buy into the values of a community that doesn't value excellence.

Step #2: Acknowledge a power greater than yourself
Trait#2: Peace of mind

Why do people believe in conspiracy theories? Because they can't bear the thought that things happen for no reason. They find it less discomfiting to believe in an evil cabal of master-manipulators, in UFOs, or in secret government programs and dark sites than to believe that *things just happen*.

There's a reason why Karl Marx disparaged religion as the "opiate of the people." Marx was correct that the masses will turn to the most outlandish explanations to make the unknown less frightening and impose order on confusion.

But that doesn't mean we have to concede to chaos.

The design of the universe testifies to organization and order. By doing so, it contradicts the Second Law of Thermodynamics. Indeed, if the universe tends toward disorder, as Newton observed, then there is no explanation for how we got here in the first place.

So whether you believe in God or intelligent design or the mystic power of the Universe, whether you call it fate or karma or kismet or mazal, there is ample empirical evidence and rationale for believing in a higher power or, at the very least, a higher purpose.

And that is comforting indeed. Because if there is a plan for the universe, then each and every one of us is part of that plan; which means that we matter, and so does the way we conduct ourselves, the way we present ourselves, and everything we do.

CHAPTER 3

Go Find a New Window

How to Make the Ordinary Extraordinary

You ordered a top sirloin at a five-star restaurant and the waiter brings you prime rib by mistake. Or you arrive on time for your reservation and still have to wait 20 minutes to get a table. Or you ask for a beer with your dinner and, after you've reminded the waiter twice, he informs you as you're finishing your meal that the restaurant is out of your selection.

Do you complain to the manager, or do you wax philosophic and chalk up the experience to the vagaries of life?

It may depend on whether you're dining cross-country or dining across town.

That's what researchers from Temple University, Arizona State University, and the University of Minnesota concluded when they studied a cross-section of restaurant reviews: we're more likely to be critical of establishments when we're closer to home than we are when we're on the road.

The question, of course, is why?

According to NPR's Shankar Vedantam, it may be that we acquire an entirely different outlook when we travel. It's not only that we expect the unexpected; we may actually *welcome* it as part of the novelty that makes us want to travel in the first place.

Conversely, our higher standards at home derive from the familiarity of our surroundings and our subconscious prediction that the future will conform to what we've experienced in the past. We are less receptive to variation when we're on home turf, since we think we know what's coming. Conversely, the spirit of adventure we feel on the road makes us more flexible and adaptable, more able to focus on what we like and filter out anything that doesn't go our way.

Another possible explanation is that we *want* to romanticize our adventures. If we've traveled hundreds or thousands of miles, we don't want to think of our trip as wasted or ill-spent, so we subconsciously augment our experiences in order to remember them as having been worth the trouble and the cost. Closer to home, we want to learn from our mistakes so that we won't repeat them; therefore, the negatives may stand out and overshadow the good.

All of which may provide us with an insight that extends far beyond going out to eat.

Consider the buzz that surrounds visiting speakers, visiting bands, visiting theater groups, and visiting comics. If a celebrity arrives from out of town, how much more excitement is generated than we find by any local personality?

Certainly, there's no guarantee that the out-of-towner will prove more engaging or enthralling than someone homegrown. But the buzz of excitement stems from the transience of the opportunity. This is something new. This is something out of the ordinary. This is a once-in-a-lifetime chance.

Will it live up to the buzz? Our subconscious minds are determined to make sure that it will.

That can be a good thing. We enjoy our experiences more because we're more invested in having them turn out well. Our anticipation is heightened before and we retain more pleasant memories after, improving our moods and increasing our feelings of joy and satisfaction.

But then there's the flip side. Our dissatisfaction with the routine, with the ordinary, with the day-to-day grind can sour our outlook on life whenever we aren't involved in novelty. And since most of life *is* routine, it's oh-so-easy to allow dark clouds to gather over our disposition and color everything in our lives with dreary shades of gray.

We get bored with our jobs, with our clothes, with our cars, with our homes. We grow indifferent towards our spouses and resentful of their imperfections, until our eyes begin to wander and our minds begin wonder if we wouldn't be happier with someone or something else. We become frustrated with our kids and wish they would stop demanding so much of the time and energy that we want to invest in living our lives.

The sad truth is that we end up missing out on our lives because we don't recognize the novelty of each new day, we don't appreciate the value of the predictable, we don't cherish the gift of the ordinary. When we can't escape to faraway places, we escape into the fantasy of movies and television, of video games and romantic novels. We trade the solid satisfaction of the real for the whimsical dream-world of imagination.

In the worst scenarios, we trade reality for fantasy and end up left with nothing at all.

So how do we keep the familiar from becoming contemptible? How do we bring a sense of newness and freshness into our humdrum lives?

Back in the fifties, a rabbinic scholar took his first trip on a jet plane. Outside the cabin window, he beheld the curvature of the earth, the clouds and the sea, and the sunrise breaking over the horizon through the darkness of the heavens. When he returned home, he told his rabbi how inspired he had been, and how he felt he had come face to face with the Divine Presence.

"I know just what you mean," his rabbi replied. "I feel exactly the same way every time I see a daisy."

Sure, there are plenty of ways we can spice up the ordinary. Candlelit dinners, moonlight walks in the park, drives in the countryside, family get-togethers, and spontaneous little adventures.

But we make a mistake when we value the extraordinary over the ordinary. True, gravy makes the turkey taste better, icing sweetens the cake, and the gleaming paint job fills us with pleasure as we get into our new car. But would we ever want gravy without the turkey or icing without the cake? And how much pleasure do we find in the polished paint job when the engine won't turn over? We get so caught up in the extras that we forget about what really gives substance and meaning to our existence.

The best way to keep life fresh is not by changing the way we live but by changing the way we look at the events that fill our lives. To spend a few moments each morning and evening giving thanks for our husbands, wives, children, parents, families, and friends; to recount the blessings of good health, a job, food on our table, a roof over our heads; to reflect upon our modest but meaningful accomplishments and to take pleasure in the little ways we contribute to our world and make it a better place, even as we look ahead toward greater accomplishments and the legacy we hope to leave behind.

Life isn't meant to be a party. It's meant to be something better, something that lasts, something that continues to fill us with joy when the parties are all over, after the fireworks are finished, once we've paid the check for dinner and return to the routine we share with the people we love.

Practical Applications – _Dos_ and _Don'ts_

- Do enjoy new and novel experiences.
- Don't discount the value of the familiar and the routine.

- Do express appreciation for everyday gifts.
- Don't overvalue the unusual or the unexpected.

- Do look for the blessings of reality as it is.
- Don't get lost in dreams and imagination.

- Do focus more on what things are and what they mean.
- Don't place too much emphasis on how things look or what others will think of them.

- Do find a sense of purpose in what you're doing now.
- Don't forget where you are because you're wishing you were somewhere else.

Step #3: Commit yourself to a higher purpose
Trait #3: Enthusiasm

What is the secret of happiness? Purpose. The most depressing thought is that nothing you do matters, that when you pass from this earth you will leave nothing behind.

That's why we turn to novels and movies to provide a sense of adventure and romance. But fiction and fantasy can steal from us our respect for convention, our trust in stability, and the value we have in the day-to-day routine of life.

If you think back to adventures you may have had in your life, you will likely find that they were much more fulfilling and gratifying in hindsight than they were when they took place, that you enjoy telling them over as stories far more than you enjoyed living through them in the moment.

It is the thrill of the unexpected and the unpredictable that compels adolescents to abandon dependable friendships for a chance at impressing the cool kids, that drives husbands and wives to cheat on each other, that convinces employees to leave stable careers for the whimsical promise of new frontiers.

Of course, we should have dreams. We should seek new experiences and look to broaden our horizons. But the very nature of our dreams and aspirations will change when we feel part of something greater than ourselves, when we define ourselves not as individuals but as partners in a noble mission, in a worthy cause, in the epic battle of good against evil.

This is why sports fans engage in such revelry when the home team wins. But their ardor cannot compare to the genuine exultation that comes from being not a spectator but a participant in a truly worthy endeavor. When a grand mission guides our efforts, we rise early, filled with zealous passion to take on each day, grateful for the opportunity to leave our mark by making the world a better place.

CHAPTER 4

Through the Windows of Confusion

Is there always safety in numbers?

"While nobody knows what's going on around here, everybody knows what's going on around here."

In his eerily prophetic 1975 novel, *The Shockwave Rider*, John Brunner describes the *Delphi pool*, a futuristic incarnation of the Las Vegas betting boards. It works this way:

Ask large numbers of people questions to which they can't possibly know the answers. For example: *How many victims died from influenza in the epidemic of 1918?*

Even though few of the subjects know anything at all about the question, their guesses will cluster around the correct answer. In the novel, the principle held true even for things that hadn't happened yet, creating a reasonably accurate window into the future.

Mr. Brunner's fantasy has a basis in reality. In 1987, finance professor Jack Treynor asked 56 students to guess the number of jelly beans in a glass jar. The average of the guesses was 871, a mere 2.5% off the actual number of 850 beans. Only one student guessed closer than the class as a whole.

This means that all of us together are smarter than all of us individually. We really are greater than the sum of our parts, and the answer to any problem often is already in the room. That's why good leaders solicit and encourage the opinions of others before expressing their own.

But it's not all good news. In a recent series of experiments, marketing professor Gita Johar of Columbia University and her team discovered something profoundly disturbing:

People are more likely to accept unverified reports as true when in the company of others than when they are by themselves.

More compelling still is that the company we keep doesn't have to be *physical* to impair our natural skepticism. Even in a social media setting – connected only *virtually* with other people – we are more likely to accept information at face value, especially if it fits in with our preconceived notions.

Professor Johar explains this as a manifestation of **herd mentality,** an unconscious response to the belief that there is safety in numbers. We don't feel the need to question or fact-check because we rely on the group for authentication, even as everyone one else in the group simultaneously relies on everyone else in the group.

Welcome to the modern Delphi pool for the dissemination of misinformation. **The more people who hear a report, the more likely they are to believe it.** In no time at all, news becomes accepted as fact regardless of accuracy, even when it is easily verifiable as false.

With groupthink becoming the standard of our times, we not only become less able to recognize the truth – we become less interested in doing so. We condemn reports as fake news *not* because they are factually incorrect but because they refuse to conform to our own version of reality. As long as we keep company with others who are similarly disinterested in the difference between true and false, we have no reason to question the status quo.

In fact, probing for the truth can be positively dangerous. One word against the party line is guaranteed to bring down upon our heads the wrath of the ignorant majority among our own allies, those determined to hold fast to fabulist misconceptions created in the ideological echo-chamber of groupthink.

Of course, we want to have and to be team players. **But a team only wins when it is made up of distinct individuals playing differentiated positions.**

This is why it's so important to encourage opposing points-of-view, and for debating parties to demonstrate an ability to articulate the opinions *of their disputants* with accuracy. If we don't examine all sides of an issue, how can we possibly know who's right and who's wrong? If we are all nodding in agreement with a predetermined conclusion, how can we identify flaws in our plan or recognize that there might be a better way of doing things?

Whenever emotions begin to overrule reason, we have to ask ourselves a question: do we want to arrive at the best possible solution, or have we become too invested in our own way of thinking to want our views disrupted by the truth?

King Solomon says, *A sophomoric person believes every word, but an insightful person minds his every step.*

If we want to live in reality, we have to break away from the delusions of the herd and follow the path that leads back to the real world. **Easy answers and simplistic solutions gain popular approval because they create an illusion of security and order.** This is why logical fallacies abound – like either/or arguments, circular reasoning, generalization, and moral equivalence.

Solving difficult problems requires determined effort and honest evaluation. If we want meaningful answers, we have to be willing to ask hard questions – and then we have to be able to face up to the truth no matter how uncomfortable or how unpopular that might make us.

Practical Applications – *Dos* and *Don'ts*

- Do ask questions, even when you think you know the answers.
- Don't discourage discussion, even when everyone seems to be in agreement.

- Do seek out dissenting voices.
- Don't repress contrarian opinions, especially when you belong to the majority.

- Do evaluate new information with a healthy dose of skepticism.
- Don't assume something is true just because most people think it is.

- Do give yourself time for private reflection over new ideas or information.
- Don't buy into data or "logic" just because it confirms your preconceptions.

- Do verify stories and data before you repeat them.
- Don't assume that others' good intentions make them reliable sources of information.

Step #4: Articulate your errors
Trait #4: Truthfulness

Have you ever found yourself arguing ferociously in defense of your point of view when, all of a sudden, it occurs to you that you are wrong and you antagonist is right?

What did you do?

If you're like most people, there's a good chance that you started arguing even harder. Or, if you couldn't rationalize continuing to defend a position you knew was wrong, you might have resorted to the popular rejoinder, "Whatever."

Human beings hate being wrong. Even more, we hate admitting we're wrong. But what would we prefer: continuing in the error of our ways, or correcting the mistake now so that we won't have an even heftier bill to pay for being wrong later?

I remember my college English professor, Max Byrd, musing that he never understood why people complain about being *disillusioned*. "I welcome the opportunity to be relieved of my illusions," the bookish professor observed.

Of course, that's the way we *should* respond. But admitting error, whether to others or to ourselves, takes courage. The longer we persist in an erroneous opinion, the more mortified we are to admit we've been wrong.

We can rationalize all we want. But a truthful person is more than just honest. Truthfulness calls for us to not only speak honestly but think honestly, to beware of such innocent lies as hasty promises, exaggeration, embellishment, and filling in stories with details that may or may not be accurate.

It also calls for us to take responsibility for our mistakes, not to fall back on that familiar political standard, "Mistakes were made."

I blew it. I messed up. It's my fault.

Admit when you're wrong, and others will respect you for your straightforwardness. They'll also be more likely to trust you when you say you're right.

CHAPTER 5

Through the Window from both Directions

How ants survive rush hour

Who doesn't hate rush hour?   Either we're stuck motionless in a sea of cars or taking our lives in our hands as if on an amusement park bumper ride.

Maybe we should take a lesson from the ants.

Yes, *ants*.

King Solomon said, *"Go, sluggard, and learn from the ant."* 28 centuries later, a physicist at the Indian Institute of Space Science and Technology took his advice.

As it turns out, ants are better drivers than we are.   By studying their highway habits, we can discover some valuable lessons that extend far beyond the way we drive.

Professor Apoorva Nagar observed that traveling ants are able to maintain a constant speed regardless of the number of ants on the road.   In other words, even at rush hour, ant traffic moves along unimpeded.

Professor Nagar suggests three possible reasons why ants don't bottleneck as traffic flow increases:

1. **Ants don't have egos.** They don't need to be first, don't need to show off, and don't take it personally when another ant cuts in front of them.
2. **Ants don't mind fender-benders.** Needless to say, a multi-ant pile-up will slow traffic to a crawl. But a few minor bumps and scrapes have little impact on their progress. Even with incidental bumping and knocking, ants just keep on moving forward.
3. **Ants get more disciplined as the crowd thickens:** they hold their speed steadier and make fewer twists and turns.

In contrast to human drivers who cut in and out while breaking and accelerating, ant discipline creates a road culture of greater predictability and, consequently, greater safety and consistency.

And although ant behavior may have limited practical application to human driving habits and traffic patterns, it may suggest other benefits to improve the quality of daily life.

Have you ever watched someone else hopelessly caught up in his own ego-gratification? It happens around the dinner table, at Little League games, and especially in the workplace. We want respect, we want credit, we want appreciation. And we often make ourselves and others miserable when we don't get them.

But when we stop worrying about our social status and stop looking for others to validate our existence, we become a lot more comfortable with where we are and end up making progress with far greater efficiency.

It's actually pretty easy once we start asking ourselves the right questions:

- What do I gain by trying to be first?
- Are the people I'm trying to impress going to be impressed?
- Are the people who are going to be impressed worth impressing?
- Didn't I read a story once about a tortoise and a hare?
- If I worry more about giving credit and respect than about getting them, isn't that the best practice for making the best impression?

To be honest, I enjoyed the frequent fantasy of trading in my vintage Camry for a new... anything. But until the old workhorse finally died, I never worried about the latest scratch, dent, or interior stain the way I would if I were driving a Mercedes... or even my new Prius.

The truth is this: the shinier our toys, the more we notice when the shine starts to fade. And when that happens, our mood fades just as quickly. That's only natural, since those scrapes and blemishes are all tied up with our first problem:

Ego.

After all, that scuffed bumper is a reflection on me.

Isn't it?

It's not just our cars. The human eye and mind seek out every imperfection on which to fixate, whether it's a loose thread or a tilted picture, a sore toe or a pesky hangnail. If anything is 99% perfect, that last one percent becomes all the more intolerable, casting a dark shadow over everything that is just the way it should be.

And that is the perfect time for another list of questions:

- Overall, are things good or bad?
- By how much does the good outweigh the bad?

- Is it reasonable to let the little that's not quite right cancel out so much that is just fine?
- Is anything every perfect?

As tension builds, we start looking for a way out. Maybe instead we should be looking for *a way in*. Like the ants who become more focused as traffic increases.

The truth is, we experience stress and tension as our bodies enter survival mode. The proper response is to heighten our awareness of the challenges that face us and steel ourselves to meet them. When we do, we propel our productivity and success to unprecedented levels by managing the job at hand, and also by increasing our ability to overcome greater obstacles that lie ahead. **It's a win-win.**

But it demands that we reframe our outlook, that we stop seeing obstacles as *impediments* to progress and start viewing them as *opportunities* for development and self-improvement. And acquiring that outlook starts with more questions:

- Why do I think *no pain, no gain* applies only at the gym?
- Haven't my most satisfying moments come through struggle?
- If I can't change what's happening to me, isn't changing how I deal with it my only other option?
- If I handle a difficult situation well, might not others follow my example and help the situation improve on its own?

After all, what's the point of an obstacle course? We could traverse the course much faster by first removing all those obstacles. But then, what would we have accomplished?

And isn't life the greatest obstacle course of all?

Practical Applications – *Dos* and *Don'ts*

- Do defer to others whenever possible.
- Don't worry about doing better than others when you're already trying to do your best.

- Do show appreciation, especially for little things.
- Don't let little scrapes keep you from enjoying the big picture.

- Do challenge yourself by pushing beyond your comfort zone.
- Don't equate comfort with tranquility or effortlessness with contentment.

- Do favor consistency and discipline over making a big splash.
- Don't worry about getting there first when you're getting there on time.

- Do focus harder when it's harder to focus.
- Don't over-fixate on the outside when the inside is doing just fine.

Step #5: Make a searching and fearless moral inventory
Trait #5: Order

When all else fails, *read the directions*. To become a brain surgeon, you start with basic chemistry and biology; a rocket scientist starts with elementary physics, and a baseball all-star starts by shagging flies. We don't like it when other people cut the line, and we shouldn't think we can do it when it comes to our careers or our relationships.

Check your ego at the door; don't worry about little bumps and bruises, especially when no harm is intended; when pressure builds, increase focus; impress others by being responsible and polite, not by one-upping them; give credit where credit is due.

Begin orderly requires first being organized, which requires inventory. What are your resources and assets? What are your liabilities and shortfalls? To be successful in business, you have to be accurate in your evaluation of where your stand before you can begin planning for where you want to go. The same is true in the business of life.

In Jim Collins business classic *Good to Great*, he presents the Stockdale Paradox: *maintain faith that you will prevail in the end while confronting the most brutal facts on the ground.*

Acknowledgment of your own shortcomings, combined with steadfast determination to improve, is the surest formula for achieving success according to every metric.

CHAPTER 6

Through the Window Darkly

Make technology your servant

July 2015. A month that will live in infamy – at least in my own mind. That was when I finally broke down and got a cell phone. I know what you're thinking: *"How did you live so long without a cell phone?"*

Let me be clear: I did not want one. I still don't. I relished my time alone and couldn't imagine the intrusive buzzing or beeping or strains of the Bee Gees interrupting my solitude – or, even worse, invading the personal space of friends and strangers alike.

A book was adequate entertainment for the doctor's waiting room; I carried phone numbers on a little notebook in my shirt pocket; and I took a real paper-and-ink shopping list to the grocery store.

But life moves on, and the virtual world closed in. The demands of work soon became irresistible. Would I take the blue pill or the red pill? Did I even have a choice?

Apparently not.

Complaints about our cell phone culture are legion, worn out, and largely ignored. But they are also true. As a society, we've grown increasingly rude, increasingly impatient, and increasingly detached from one another despite the illusion of connectedness. We are distracted at work, in school, in our cars, in church or in synagogue. Vowels are an endangered species; punctuation is irrelevant. And most of us couldn't care less.

But there's something much more insidious about the cell phone culture. Collectively, we're forgetting how to think, how to communicate, and how to genuinely connect.

Too much data; too little analysis. Too many factoids; too little verification. Too easy access to information; too little discipline turning knowledge into purposeful direction.

As a teacher, I watched year after year as my students lost their enthusiasm for learning. Too many of them stopped caring if they failed, as if some cosmic reset button would let them start the Game of Life all over again. Incredibly, often their parents didn't care either, as long as their children felt good about themselves.

Which they didn't. Happiness blossoms only from the fertile soil of purpose.

And now it's true among adults as well. Once eager minds have turned increasingly lobotomized by the endless stream of pseudo-information and imagery inundating their senses. People are less inclined to ask questions or seek answers. Curiosity has vanished. After all, why do we need to know anything when all knowledge is only a click away?

As the world becomes increasingly two-dimensional, is it any wonder that people are increasingly superficial and self-absorbed? With information measured in sound bites, with news stories reduced to headlines, with presidential debates rendered in rehearsed quips and party slogans, the virtual world is feeding us a diet of intellectual and emotional junk food that leaves our minds and our souls withered from malnutrition.

How ironic to long for the days when the great evil in the world was network television. With a mere handful of channels to watch, often a book was the best option for an evening's entertainment. No texting, no videogames, no Netflix or Hulu or YouTube. And no TiVo! We had to schedule our time around our favorite shows, and if we wanted to watch two shows scheduled simultaneously... too bad! We waited for rerun season in the spring and summer, when we might get *one* second chance.

How bizarre to long for the days of only snail mail. Writing a letter took thought and effort, and then days of waiting before it arrived. But readers of a certain age will remember a child's anticipation of mail-call at summer camp, and the excitement of getting a letter from home. Then there was the tingle of courtship by post, the hundred visions and revisions, the flutter of the heart when sealing a letter to be sent, or of unsealing it on the receiving end.

So what about me? Have I gotten sucked into the black hole of cerebral oblivion like all those who have gone before? Was I able to make the phone my servant instead of finding myself enslaved by yet another machine?

Not completely. But here are a few simple strategies that might benefit us all.

Turn it off. When you can't, shouldn't, or don't need to answer your phone – use the *off* button. That's what it's there for.

Even on vibrate, the constant reminder of connectedness disconnects us from whatever should be occupying our attention. At dinner, in a meeting, at the symphony, in synagogue or church, having a conversation with someone whose time you value... why do we want to be distracted by those ubiquitous alerts? And what are we telling others about how they rank on our scale of priorities when we keep checking our screens to see if something is "important"?

Leave it behind. Go for a walk. Read a book in the park. Make a date for lunch or dinner. And when you do, leave the phone at home or in the car.

A dog on a leash needs to know its master. A human being is a different story. And the worst part of letting our phones enslave us is that we indulge the illusion that we're still free and in control of our lives.

It will be painful at first. Everything worthwhile is, before we discover how liberating it can be.

Only use it when you need it. Okay, there's a time and place for everything... even videogames. But the real value of technology is communication.

Respond to texts and emails in a timely way. Because it's so easy to reply, disregard for those who try to communicate with you sends a clear message of disregard and disdain. It only takes a moment to let someone know you got their message and that you care enough to acknowledge it. With very little effort, you have truly become more profoundly connected. Over time, those virtual connections will pay dividends in real-life connections and relationships.

King Solomon says, *If the snake bites because it was not charmed, there is no benefit to the charmer's art*. It's tempting to try and harness great power. But the illusion that it has been harnessed does not make it so.

Remember that in *The Matrix*, the only thing that saved Keanu Reeves and the rest of humanity was a landline.

Take a technology Sabbath. In a quietly growing trend, individuals and families are logging off and shutting down for one day a week.

Instead of binge-watching Netflix or following endless threads on social media, set aside 24 hours to spend with real human beings – playing, laughing, talking, or quietly enjoying one another's presence while rediscover the ancient joy of reading a book.

Go for a walk in the park, a stroll along the beach, a swim in the pool. Play Frisbee or croquet or catch. Even household chores like raking leaves, shoveling snow, or tidying up your room can have a therapeutic effect, resetting your psyche and reminding you that technology exists to serve mankind, not enslave or infantilize us.

The discipline we can develop with a few hours abstinence will serve us well throughout each coming week, reminding us to retain our perspective, recover our self-control, and reclaim mastery over our thoughts and desires.

Practical Applications – *Dos* and *Don'ts*

- Do turn off your phone when your attention should be on a human being.
- Don't worry about calls or notices you'll miss – they'll still be there later.

- Do leave your phone behind when you know you won't need it.
- Don't become a servant to that which is supposed to serve you.

- Do show others respect by responding to them in a timely way.
- Don't interrupt people you're with to respond to people you are not with.

- Do set aside time for non-technology activities.
- Don't forget that there is a real world as well as a virtual one.

- Do invest time thinking about information.
- Don't value information over wisdom.

Step #6: Look beyond yourself; take action to improve your character
Trait #6: Diligence

Why is there such universal respect for Navy SEALs? Because we all have some idea how difficult it is to join their ranks. The combination of physical endurance, mental toughness, and iron-willed commitment has become the stuff of legend.

But the common factor that defines the most elite military forces is a quality accessible to everyone: *determination.*

When life is too comfortable, when little is demanded from us, when we search for meaning and purpose in our lives and come up empty, it's almost impossible to summon the drive necessary for achieving greatness. When the rest of the world is satisfied with mediocrity, why should we expect more from ourselves?

Commitment to a higher purpose doesn't automatically translate into peace of mind and joyful enthusiasm. We need to harness that sense of vision and mission by applying ourselves toward becoming worthy, by defining ourselves as faithful servants to an honorable cause.

The ideals of quality, of excellence, and of discipline can drive us to accomplish extraordinary feats, but only if we set our sights far beyond ourselves, only if we stretch our imaginations and awaken in our hearts the firm belief that there is no limit to what we can become.

With that mindset, and with relentless perseverance, the impossible can truly become possible.

CHAPTER 7

When the window becomes a mirror

Reclaiming Civility

A child's brain is like a sponge, absorbing everything with which it comes in contact. As the brain gets older it learns to process, to analyze, to interpret. And eventually it begins to slow, begins to forget, begins to lose function.

Few prospects are as forbidding as mental decline, the specter of which haunts us as we advance toward old age. And so the experts tell us to keep our minds active, that using the brain is the surest way to stave off mental deterioration.

- Crossword puzzles
- Sudoku
- Word games
- Logic problems

These are common recipes from the diet books for the mind. But don't stop there; the more creative and more challenging, the better for your brain.

- Go traveling
- Take up knitting or gardening

- Learn Italian
- Drive a different way to work
- Get an advanced degree

Anything and everything that piques cognitive activity belongs in our catalogue of mental health activities.

"That's all good," says Barbara Strauch, author of *The Secret Life of the Grown-Up Brain: The Surprising Talents of the Middle-Aged Mind* and *New York Times* health and medical science editor. But the most intriguing advice Ms. Strauch has heard is this:

"Deliberately challenge your view of the world. Talk to people you totally disagree with."

It makes sense. Nothing kicks the brain into overdrive like having to defend your point of view against attack, or the desire to dismantle an argument you find unsound or wrongheaded. What's more, Ms. Strauch asserts that the brain is actually primed for questioning assumptions, since reexamining our beliefs provides the opportunity to revisit, or more deeply contemplate, why we believe the way we do.

"Confronting things you disagree with may not make you change your mind," she says, "but it will perhaps give you a view that is more satisfying to the middle-aged brain."

And who knows? *Sometimes we may even discover that we've been wrong.*

Bill Bishop would almost certainly agree. In his 2008 book *The Big Sort: Why the Clustering of Like-Minded America Is Tearing Us Apart*, Mr. Bishop shows how local communities are becoming increasingly homogenous as people sort themselves into demographic cliques. The most striking irony is how the increasing singularity of ideas and values in neighborhoods across the country is resulting in increasing divisiveness throughout the country as a whole.

The statistical evidence is compelling:

The 2004 reelection of George W. Bush over John Kerry was decided nationally by one closely contested state (Ohio) and a sliver of the electorate; in the same election, almost half the counties in the country recorded landslide victories locally for either one candidate or the other, nearly double the percentage recorded in 1976.

Mr. Bishop describes how economic and geographical mobility allowed people to orient themselves around and among others who share their beliefs, values, and predilections. Members of religious and civic organizations have become increasingly uniform in their ways of thinking, particularly with respect to politics.

Citing marketing analyst J. Walker Smith, Mr. Bishop explains how a pervasive movement of "self-invention" gave rise to a desire to impose our will upon the world around us, to redefine ourselves and our environment according to our own narrow world view. According to Mr. Smith, prosperity and technology have enabled people to "wrap themselves into cocoons entirely of their own making." **We expect the world to be the way we want it to be, with no room for compromise.**

Mr. Bishop reaches the conclusion that:

> As people seek out the social settings they prefer — as they choose the group that makes them feel the most comfortable — the nation grows more politically segregated — and the benefit that ought to come with having a variety of opinions is lost to the righteousness that is the special entitlement of homogeneous groups.

We all live with the results: balkanized communities whose inhabitants find other Americans to be culturally incomprehensible; a growing intolerance for political differences that has made national consensus impossible; and politics so polarized that Congress is stymied and elections are no longer just contests over policies, but bitter choices between ways of life.

The more single-minded a group becomes in its opinions, the more calcified its thinking becomes in its evaluation of unfamiliar ideas, and the more quickly it rejects and condemns opposing viewpoints. Homogenous groups are increasingly likely to indulge in stereotyping, rationalization, complacency, peer pressure, self-censorship, a sense of moral superiority, and an appearance of unanimity that creates the illusion of invulnerability. Once-rational arguments devolve into dogma and character assassination.

The resulting groupthink has been blamed for some of history's worst snafus:

- the construction of the French Maginot line
- the Bay of Pigs fiasco
- U.S. failure to anticipate the Japanese attack on Pearl Harbor
- involvement in the Vietnam War
- the *Challenger* Space Shuttle disaster
- the financial collapse of 2008

But there really is nothing new under the sun. Nearly 3000 years ago, King Solomon anticipated this very state of affairs when he observed that, *Iron sharpens iron, and a man sharpens the mind of his fellow.*

In a world plagued by ideological self-segregation, it's easy to recognize Solomon's wisdom in comparing iron blades that sharpen one another to iron wills that hone syllogistic reasoning to a fine edge. Indeed, the great talmudic scholars of 2000 years ago debated in the tradition of Solomon, arguing with a ferocity described as fighting "with swords and spears."

Nevertheless, those same students and sages retained a level of **mutual respect** as impressive as their erudition, establishing a standard and style of scholarship that defines talmudic discourse until today.

Even with respect to practical jurisprudence, talmudic law was so concerned with legal objectivity that if the Sanhedrin, the ancient high court of 71 sages, voted for conviction in a capital case without a single dissension, the death penalty could not be given.

No matter how overwhelming the evidence, the ancients would not trust their own objectivity if none of their members could find at least one mitigating factor. By the same token, two brothers were not permitted to testify together in rabbinic court, since shared, common perspective might compromise their objectivity.

Democratic government was intended to stimulate debate, to create transparency, to hold public servants accountable to the will of the people. The democratic process was never intended to become a popularity contest in which candidates pander to voters or attempt to manipulate them with scare tactics or empty rhetoric. Even its most ardent supporters were never blind to its shortcomings, as is clear from Winston Churchill's remark that,

Democracy is the worst form of government, except for all those other forms that have been tried from time to time.

Nevertheless, with literally billions of dollars now spent on marketing, sloganeering, parodies, and sound bites – not to mention bitter and violent partisanship – it's hard not to conclude that the system is broken. If we want to have any hope for real change, we have to be willing to understand the other side before we condemn it.

And the same applies in our families, our jobs, and our communities – anywhere we hope to flourish and prosper.

Excerpted and adapted from *Proverbial Beauty: Secrets for Success and Happiness from the Wisdom of the Ages*

Practical Applications – *Dos* and *Don'ts*

- Do argue, respectfully, even if your opinion is unpopular.
- Don't take a position just because you think others will support you in it.

- Do question assertions that seem weak in facts or logic.
- Don't keep quiet, just because you are not confident in your opinion.

- Do thoughtfully consider arguments that challenge your preconceptions.
- Don't be afraid of being wrong.

- Do offer evidence to defend your position that addresses challenges from the other side.
- Don't be defensive when your point-of-view is challenged.

- Do respond to irrational or unsupported arguments from others with polite firmness.
- Don't remain noncommittal to avoid tension and conflict.

Step #7: Listen to understand the positions held by others
Trait #7: Silence

The 18th century French essayist Joseph Joubert said, "It is better to debate a question without settling it than to settle a question without debating it."

If you can't explain why others believe what they believe, how can you be sure they're wrong? And if you can't articulate why they might reasonably disagree with you, how can you be sure you're right?

If all we want to do is wait our turn to speak so we can propound our own beliefs, then we aren't engaging in conversation or discussion. We are practicing what my college psychology professor liked to call *dialogues of the deaf*. This kind of self-indulgent rhetoric is worse than useless, since we end up convincing no one other than ourselves, regardless of whether we are right or wrong.

In ancient times, when the Jewish high court of sages debated matters of law, it was the least distinguished of the scholars who spoke first. This ensured that everyone present would offer his own opinion without any pressure to conform to the majority or fear of contradicting a more respected sage.

CEOs and team leaders are well advised to employ this practice, to make every member of the team feel valued and to allow every point-of-view due consideration.

As we have already observed, the same letters the make up the world *listen* also make up the word *silent*.

CHAPTER 8

Your Neighbor's Window

When in doubt... just ask!

Does this sound familiar?

You're running out the door to take your wife to the airport, only to discover you have a flat tire. You don't have time to wait for a taxi or the auto club. You want to ask your neighbor for a ride, but you're afraid it's too much of an imposition.

Or... you see someone on the subway reading a book by your favorite author or about a topic you find fascinating. You want to strike up a conversation, but you're afraid of intruding on the other person's privacy.

Or... you have a lead on a promising job opportunity, and an acquaintance has dealings with your prospective employer. You want to ask her to make an introduction, but you don't want to put her in an uncomfortable position.

Maybe you're afraid of rejection; maybe you're afraid of overstepping the bounds of the relationship; maybe you're afraid of being a pest.

Sure, there are boundaries, and sometimes we do cross them. So if these scenarios arise often, you might need to examine whether you're overly needy.

But most of us aren't looking for such situations; they just happen. And when they do, here's the key: *just ask!* You'll recognize the benefits almost immediately.

It feels good. There's a reason why "it never hurts to ask" is such an enduring cliché. Most people are more than happy to help a friend in need, to respond to polite solicitations, or to put themselves out for others. It's a truism of human psychology that we feel better – both about ourselves and about others – when we give than when we take.

In fact, a study at Canada's Simon Fraser University found that children as young as two years old experienced greater pleasure from giving than they did from getting. According to this research, the impulse to give is hardwired into our nature.

So it really is better to give than to receive. Consequently, the greatest gift you can give someone else is the opportunity to give.

And what's the worst that can happen? If they say no, you're no worse off than you were before. And then you can offer someone else the chance to give.

It brings us closer. If someone says yes, you may find that you've forged a closer bond or made a new friend. Benjamin Franklin described how, after asking to borrow a rare book from a rival in the Pennsylvania legislature, he found that his colleague's demeanor changed from cool indifference to warm camaraderie.

What's more, others may actually want us to reach out to them. A University of Chicago study showed that commuters on the subway are happier to pass the time chatting with a stranger than sitting in solitude. But most of them – most of us – sit in isolation, too worried about how people might react if we violate their space or their privacy.

How do you feel when someone asks how you're doing and genuinely wants to know? Or can you remember the last time it happened?

By reaching out to people, whether with real interest or just with a smile and a "good morning," we brighten up their world and, ultimately, our own.

It's the way of wisdom. Gerry Spence, one of the most successful trial lawyers in America, explains it this way:

"I have learned [more] from my dogs than from all the great books I have read. The wisdom of my dog is the product of his inability to conceal his wants. There are no games. No professor told me that I might live a more successful life if I simply ask for love... when I needed it."

Human beings are social creatures, and we're at our best when we engage others. So why deprive others of the chance to engage us?

And why deprive yourself of the chance to get what you need?

It's the key to success. The same principle applies in the workplace. We may be afraid that a boss or coworker will interpret a question as a sign of incompetence; in truth, the willingness to ask for help or seek counsel will lead us on the pathway to improved performance and impress others with our team spirit.

Bestselling business author Bernard Marr sums it up like this:

"Successful people never rest on the belief that they know everything possible. They put a premium on investing in themselves through education and training." And that includes asking for advice when we need it. He then quotes Gandhi: "Live as if you were to die tomorrow. Learn as if you were to live forever."

You never know. As she was working on *Getting There: A Book of Mentors*, Gillian Zoe Segal took inspiration from Sara Blakely, who camped out in reception rooms before convincing a hosiery manufacturer to produce the prototype for Spanx, the product that launched her billion-dollar career. Ms. Segal describes how she plucked up the courage to approach Warren Buffett at a charity event and, in 15 seconds, opened the door to an interview with the Oracle of Omaha for her book, which became a bestseller.

Does it seem insane to approach one of the world's richest men and ask for a favor? Of course, it does. But that doesn't mean it might not pay off in the end.

The Talmud teaches that *a bashful person will never become wise*. If we are afraid to ask, we cannot learn and grow. And if we don't learn and grow, chances are that we will never succeed.

Whether we are need of information, advice, assistance, or simple companionship, the solution is often as easy as asking. And if someone says *no*, don't take it personally. There's a whole world of people out there waiting to say *yes*.

All you have to do is ask.

Practical Applications – *Dos* and *Don'ts*

- Do ask for help when you need it, and sometimes even when you don't.
- Don't assume others are doing fine just because they act like they are.

- Do look for signs that others may need help and ask what you can do.
- Don't be too quick to take no for an answer; sometimes people need help to accept help.

- Do show concern for others with a smile, a greeting, and by taking genuine interest.
- Don't contribute to others feeling ignored or neglected.

- Do look for opportunities to learn from more knowledgeable people.
- Don't be afraid to approach people who might be able to help you.

- Do encourage collaboration and give others the chance to share in your success.
- Don't see coworkers as competitors.

Step #8: Articulate the ideas of others so they know they have been heard
Trait #8: Respect

We show respect for others by demonstrating appreciation for their value. This can take the form of asking for their help and soliciting their advice. People want to feel that they make a difference, that they are making a contribution, that their voices are heard.

And the more we show respect for others, the more reason they have to respect us.

In fact, the best way to win an argument is to first find something in the other person's position to agree with. The moment we validate an antagonist, whether through acknowledging they are right or just demonstrating we understand their position, we begin to transform the exchange from a debate into a conversation.

Once that happens, we are no long combatants seeking victory over one another but partners in pursuit of truth.

Moreover, by validating some element in an opposing position, we reframe our own perspective and become more receptive to the possibility that there may be other aspects of that position worth considering.

We've already observed that all of us are smarter than any of us, which means that the answer is often already in the room. Refusing to listen and understand opposing positions is a waste of wisdom. Even if an opinion turns out to be wrong, giving it reasonable consideration will help clarify the correct alternative.

And sometimes, what we thought was wrong turns out to be right.

CHAPTER 9

Seeing Through the Window of your Mind

Three tips for programming your moral GPS

There's a popular phrase that perfectly describes driving in Israel: *near-death experience.*

In some ways it's better than it used to be. Traffic has gotten so dense that drivers simply cannot indulge the reckless habits that once prevailed. It's hard to bob and weave when your car is stuck in gridlock.

But when the traffic starts moving, the experience can be harrowing, made all the more stressful as you try to find your way along unfamiliar boulevards and react by making quick turns with little notice.

So thank heaven for Waze. Just plug in your destination, follow the directions, and *voila!*

Then something strange happened. A few days into our visit, I noticed that my wife – who had the good sense to leave all the driving to me – was telling me which way to go moments before I heard the same instructions from the polite voice of the GPS.

After travelling many of the same routes to and from our rented apartment, my wife had learned her way around from the passenger seat while I had given myself over so completely to the computer that I was utterly lost without a female voice to guide me.

Is technology a metaphysical response to mankind's diminishing capacity? Or is our dependence upon every new technology responsible for our intellectual decline? Maybe both are true. But either way, there is no denying that dependence on technology begets ever greater dependence.

Of course, it's not a problem until our battery dies or the grid goes down. But when that happens, our inability to manage on our own leaves us crippled, if not paralyzed. We don't need a dog to eat our homework anymore. A malfunctioning cell tower or a faulty modem provides a ready-made excuse for any failure.

But there may be a more positive lesson in all this. Just like some people are born with a natural sense of direction, almost everyone is born with an instinctive moral compass. We commonly refer to this as our *conscience*. But what exactly is it?

- the inner arbiter of right and wrong?
- the angelic figure hovering over one shoulder?
- the pang of guilt we feel when we cross over the dividing line between what we *want* to do and what we *ought* to do?

Any of these might be correct. But where does conscience come from? Why does one person's conscience steer him in a different direction from another's? And why do we find it so difficult to follow where our conscience wants to lead us?

Sigmund Freud famously divided the human psyche into three components. The **id** is the sense of self, the seat of survival instincts, personal desire, and immediate physical gratification. The **ego** is our concern for how we are seen by others, for social acceptance, for power and influence. The **superego** is the conscience, forever embattled trying to rein in the other two impulses and keep them on the straight and narrow.

In short, the conscience is our moral GPS. It is our universal guidance system for living meaningful and ethical lives.

And just like the GPS that tells us which street or avenue to follow, so too the voice of the conscience can become weakened when we don't update the software, when we travel into dead zones, when we lower the volume, or when we turn it off altogether.

So here are three simple tips for keeping our conscience clear and on target.

Start with authority. Since we go to experts for medical advice, legal advice, and auto repair advice, why do we presume to be experts ourselves when it comes to moral and spiritual well-being? Throughout the ages, purveyors of wisdom have pondered the definitions of good and evil, attempting to aid those of us who seek to find our way.

So don't try to go it on your own, and beware of charlatans who espouse virtue for the advancement of their own agendas. As Sir Isaac Newton said, *If I have seen farther, it is because I stand on the shoulders of giants.*

The mind and the heart are often in conflict. Generally speaking, the mind is a more reliable adviser than the heart. But that's only generally speaking. Human capacity for rationalization is limitless: we are exceptionally talented at finding reasons for doing what we want to do and highly practiced at ignoring that inner voice when it whispers that we are about to take a wrong turn.

So we have to do our best to evaluate our actions before we act, to re-evaluate them after we act so we can be better prepared for next time, and to continually recalculate as long our the head and our heart remain at odds with one another.

The majority is not always right. The world used to be flat. The sun used to revolve around the earth. Man was not meant to fly. That's how it was, until it wasn't. And so it was – and is – concerning matters of equality and justice. Just because a belief is widely held does not make it right.

The less willing people are to question or debate their own beliefs, the more reason there is to suspect that their reasoning may be flawed. As the French essayist Joseph Joubert said: *It's better to debate a question without settling it than to settle a question without debating it.*

No one ever said it was easy to do the right thing. But the harder we try, the better we become. And as we become better, we make the world we live in a better place as well.

Practical Applications – *Dos* and *Don'ts*

- Do study classical ethics and moral philosophy.
- Don't assume that you can reason or "feel" your way to what's right on your own.

- Do discuss both sides of an issue with others before making decisions.
- Don't tell yourself it's time wasted if you don't reach a meeting of minds.

- Do have the courage to question popular or stylish thinking.
- Don't follow the crowd just because it's easier or safer.

- Do listen to both your reason and your intuition.
- Don't stop questioning yourself until your mind and your heart are at peace with each other.

- Do revisit value decisions from time to time.
- Don't assume that something is right just because you've always done it that way.

Step #9: Confront personal bias and emotion
Trait #9: Justice

What color is a yield sign? If you're over 40, there's a good chance you answered *yellow*.

You might be astonished when you Google "yield sign" and discover that those signs are actually red on the outside and white in the middle. If you're like me, you will ask incredulously, *"When did this happen?"*

You will then be even more flummoxed to discover that yield signs changed from yellow to red in 1971 – half a century ago.

This is the power of preconception: when we "know" something, we refuse to question it, even when hard evidence confronts us at nearly every turn.

If this phenomenon holds true for a matter as inconsequential as the color of a traffic sign, how much more so for our deep-set beliefs, personal prejudices, business proposals, and political opinions?

If we don't recognize how emotionally invested we are in our ideas and ideologies, we will never consider the possibility that we may be wrong, or that those who think otherwise might be right.

If we want to ensure that justice is on our side, we need to follow the poker-player's first rule of competition and *leave emotion at the door.* We can try to bluff our way through by acting self-assured; but how much better to actually hold a winning hand by discarding the biases of youth and drawing from the deck of authentic knowledge and genuine wisdom?

CHAPTER 10

The Window to the Soul

Staying honest in a dishonest world

Who doesn't like a good story?

After spending my prodigal youth hitchhiking cross country and circling the globe, after a decade living abroad and over 20 years teaching and lecturing diverse audiences across the country, I have a few stories to tell.

But it still happens that friends and neighbors occasionally respond to my recollections by asking: "Did that *really* happen?"

Are my tales so truly unbelievable? I never claimed to have helped Edison invent the light bulb or to have masterminded the Normandy invasion.

I've merely looked for the story within the story, plucking insights from slightly quirky encounters and offering a bit of wisdom from my observations on the human condition.

"I loved your article," someone will say. And then, predictably: "Did that really happen?"

I even get it from my mother.

To be honest, it should come as no surprise. After all, honesty has seen its market value tumble over the years with countless reports of plagiarism, factual carelessness, and blatant fabrication.

But as troubling as such prevarication may be from the media, it's far more disheartening when it becomes the norm among our political leaders.

The sad truth is that we expect our politicians to lie. But the brazenness with which they conjure up easily verifiable falsehoods grows ever more astonishing.

Once integrity disappears, the only motive *not* to lie is fear of not getting away with it — and in a society that has grown indifferent to lying, there are rarely consequences for even the most brazen untruths.

And that has consequences for all of us.

But there is something we can do. Here are ten ways we can prevent the erosion of our own integrity:

Don't exaggerate

- "I could have *died*."
- "I've said it a *million* times."
- "You *never* listen when I talk to you."

These may seem harmless, but every exaggeration makes us a little less sensitive to honesty and authenticity.

Disciplining ourselves to speak accurately reinforces respect for the truth, both in ourselves and in those who hear us.

Don't embellish. How many popular motion pictures "based on" or "inspired by" true stories are guilty of wild embellishments that distort fact into Hollywood fiction?

How often do we ourselves add details to make a good story "better?"

But consider what it says about us — *and what it teaches our children* — when the truth isn't good enough.

Don't look for loopholes. When we use truth as a means of deception, it becomes an even more perverse form of falsehood. Like the employee in Isaac Asimov's short story "Truth to Tell," who swore that he did not steal either "the cash **or** the bonds" when in fact he had stolen the cash **and** the bonds.

And will we ever forget the presidential defense of perjury that rested on "what the definition of *is* is"?

The *letter of the law* becomes irrelevant when we no longer respect the *spirit of the law.*

Know your facts. If you don't know — or can't remember — the details of a story, *don't make them up.*

Again, it might seem irrelevant; it might even *be* irrelevant. But commitment to Truth is never irrelevant.

If a story isn't worth telling without details you don't have, don't bother telling it at all. Presenting uncertainty as fact only adds fuel to the spreading wildfire of moral confusion.

And remember what Mark Twain said: *If you tell the truth, you don't have to remember anything.*

Be a skeptic. Have you heard some interesting news? What's the source? A forwarded email? Conservative talk radio? MSNBC? Fox news? NPR? Most outlets have some bias or agenda. And some are outright fraudulent.

Before repeating a story, do your homework and make sure it's credible. Over time, it's possible to determine which new services and which reporters can be trusted.

And always keep in mind that there are two sides to every story.

Admit ignorance. It's okay not to know something. But to claim knowledge when you know you don't know is irresponsible — and usually comes back to bite you.

There's no shame in admitting a lack of knowledge, especially when followed up with a sincere promise to do some research and fill in the gaps.

Remember what Aristophanes said: *Ignorance can be educated, but stupid last forever.*

And remember what else Mark Twain said: *Better to remain silent and be thought a fool than to speak and remove all doubt.*

Admit guilt. We all make mistakes. Acknowledging error promptly and attempting to correct damage swiftly is one of the surest signs of integrity.

How many personal and political crises blossomed out of momentary lapses that grew into scandalous cover-ups?

When we admit guilt, we model character and responsibility to those around us. We also help our own cause: by acknowledging guilt when we are guilty, we earn others' trust when we declare our innocence.

Avoid liars. Behavior is contagious.

The more we associate with people who don't care about the truth, the more likely we are to stop caring about it ourselves.

Avoid political correctness. This doesn't mean we shouldn't be civil. Good manners are always in order, and many people still find profanity offensive.

But resorting to ludicrous euphemisms because someone somewhere might take offense is just another way of obfuscating truth. We should treat the janitor with respect because he provides an essential service, not because he's a "sanitation engineer." There's no insult in calling things what they are.

Look for the good. Honesty doesn't require us to say everything we know or anything we think. Sometimes, honesty is definitely the *wrong* policy, as in the case of malicious gossip or hurtful, personal remarks.

However, with a little creativity we can avoid conflicts between truth and etiquette.

If we exercise more caution with our own words, we might be less suspicious of those stories about little miracles and inspirational irony that make our eyes sparkle and our hearts swell.

And if a more profound commitment to honesty helps us become less cynical and more easily inspired, think how much good that will do for us and for the people who share our lives.

As King David writes in Psalms: *Would you be one who desires life, who loves days of seeing good? Guard your tongue from evil, and your lips from speaking falsehood.*

Practical Applications – *Dos* and *Don'ts*

- Do stick to the facts.
- Don't embellish or exaggerate to make stories more "interesting."

- Do take care to associate with honest people.
- Don't assume that poor character is not contagious.

- Do be civil and courteous at all times.
- Don't indulge in political correctness by refusing to call things what they are.

- Do admit when you aren't sure or made a mistake.
- Don't manipulate truth to escape responsibility.

- Do train yourself to focus on the good.
- Don't fully trust until you've had the chance to verify.

Step #10: Reject double standards and
Intellectual inconsistency
Trait #10: Cleanliness

It's not unusual to find two opposing points of view that can each be defended with sound, logical reasoning. When that happens, two ideological adversaries can debate one another without reaching any resolution, agree to disagree, and part respectfully as friends.

So when do problems arise? In the case where either antagonist reverses his application of logic when the same situation falls out on the other side of the philosophical divide.

It is this kind of disingenuous thinking that has given politics and politicians such a bad name. Proponents of divergent views often appear either unaware or unconcerned when they advocate positions based on the same argument that they vociferously rejected when the issue at hand opposed their own agenda.

Popular contempt for politics and politicians is the inevitable consequence of this kind of double-think. Employees lose respect for bosses and colleagues in the face of intellectual inconsistency. Relationships of every kind erode when trust is compromised by shifting logic and disregard for facts.

The same infuriating double-standards are all too common in every arena of human interaction. If we want to be free from the perversion of rationalization, we need to remain aware of our biases, consistent in our thinking, and honest with ourselves.

CHAPTER 11

Doors and Windows

Post-victory let-downs are for the birds

In the name of science, I'd like to propose a new study to investigate how researchers choose their topics. If my proposal finds acceptance, Jessica Stagner of the University of Florida will almost certainly figure prominently in the investigation.

Professor Stagner and her colleagues hoped to find support for evidence indicating that gamblers feel the same thrill of excitement when they *almost* win as they do when they *actually* win. To do so, they created an experiment in which pigeons had to peck at colored markers in order to receive hidden rewards.

That's right: *Pigeons*.

And what was their conclusion? Pigeons are smarter than people.

At least that's the way NPR's Shankar Vedantam sums it up. In more technical language, the researchers believe that a near-miss creates the illusion that we have control over situations that are largely random. This is similar to the hypothesis that people embrace conspiracy theories because they find a world manipulated by sinister puppet-masters less frightening than one in which events unfold for no reason at all, or in which the universe just doesn't care.

This should come as no surprise. As technology places more and more power in our hands, we feel less capable of controlling that technology and more at the mercy of others who are better able to manipulate it. The *illusion* that we are in control offsets the anxiety of events swirling around us faster than we can handle or process them. By the same token, the faintest whiff of victory calms our troubled souls and allows us to indulge the fantasy that success is just within our grasp.

But there may be a more profound lesson to these studies. Because, in one sense, the mere prospect of success truly is more satisfying than success itself.

Do you remember the last time you were engaged in a really engrossing novel, a gripping action movie, a challenging business project, or a date on which all the chemistry was just right? Do you remember the excitement, the elation of living in the moment, the expectation of what was to come?

And do you remember the bittersweet commingling of fulfillment and disappointment when it was over?

In truth, we love *winning* much more than we love to *have won*.

Why? Because at the very moment of success, victory, conquest, or completion, we have to face the inevitable question: *what do we do next?*

How much more do we enjoy the keen pleasure of watching success draw near, of feeling the approach of victory? And even when things don't go our way in the end, we can still bask in the glow of that tantalizing instant when we felt victory waiting right around the corner.

The mistake we so often make is to focus on our goals with such single-mindedness that we forget to enjoy the *process* of attaining them. The first day of an adventure is usually the most exciting, for it is filled with possibility and mystery, while every successive day brings us closer to the moment when it will all be over.

And what is life but our greatest adventure? Which, of course, is why so many of us are terrified of it coming to an end. But if we infuse every possible instant with the thrill of what might be, then all our days will be filled with the fragrance, if not the reality, of success, and all our moments will be filled with the happiness that comes from the pursuit of purpose.

This is what King Solomon meant when he said, *Fortunate is the one who listens for me, attentively waiting at my doors day by day, keeping watch by the doorposts of my entryways.*

Less exciting than what we find on the other side of each door is the *anticipation* of the next opportunity and the next challenge, of looking forward to each success not as an end unto itself but as a stepping stone to the success that will follow and every one that will follow after that.

Indeed, the purveyors of Jewish mysticism refer to spiritual levels as *steps*, because the moment we reach the top of one step we immediately find ourselves at the bottom of the next one.

Indeed, once we make it to the rooftop, we find ourselves nowhere but in the company of pigeons.

The ladder of success is scaled neither by stepping on those beneath us nor by pulling down those above us, but by recalibrating the measure of true achievement, by setting benchmarks of intrinsic value, and by appreciating that the determined pursuit of lofty goals is itself the loftiest goal of all.

Practical Applications – *Dos* and *Don'ts*

- Do savor the process.
- Don't miss the journey because you're fixated on the destination.

- Do find value in small victories.
- Don't overvalue the attainment of any objective.

- Do plan out both short-term and long-term goals.
- Don't expect completion of any task to give you an enduring sense of fulfillment.

- Do see short-term failures as an opportunity for renewed effort.
- Don't assume that others are plotting against you when success does not come quickly or easily.

- Do look to challenge yourself with increasingly demanding jobs.
- Don't imagine that there is some ultimate goal that will bring you everlasting happiness.

Step #11: *Through self-reflection and meditation, seek deeper awareness of purpose, knowledge of truth, and the wisdom to implement them in your life*

Trait #11: **Patience**

Do you remember the last time you read a really good book, the kind you could hardly bring yourself to put down? Do you remember the excitement you felt as you approached the end, the tension of conflict and the anticipation of resolution?

Now, can you remember how you felt moments after completing the last page? The let down, the lack of direction, the rudderless feeling of *what's next*?

We often suffer from the delusion that life is a series of projects to complete, of milestones to achieve, and of victories to be won. We focus on each perceived destination to the extent that we fail to experience the journey.

Psychologists have long recognized the benefits of mindfulness and meditation, making time to clear our thoughts from the endless items on our to-do lists and simply focusing on our breathing or contemplating all we have to be grateful for.

But meditation has an additional benefit: it builds the mental discipline that teaches patience. The urgency we feel to complete the next job and the next after that blinds to the arc or our lives and the ultimate purpose of our existence – to be good and do good.

Wisdom and virtue are a long game. Fleeting victories feel good in the moment, but they play little part in the attainment of true success.

CHAPTER 12

Keep the Window Open

Ten tips for a safer, healthier workplace

Here we are again, shaking our collective heads the latest harassment headlines. How did this happen? How did we get here? For how long will these stories continue to surface?

But the question we should be asking is: what can *we* do about it? Here are a few common-sense curatives for the pandemic of predators in the workplace.

Don't go it alone. Vice President Mike Pence was widely mocked and ridiculed after disclosing that he doesn't dine alone with any woman other than his wife. But there is safety in numbers, and the mere presence of a third party reminds us to behave better. By keeping private interactions semi-public, you're less likely to end up in a compromising position.

No flirting. Sure, it's fun. Like a little kid whisking his finger through a flame, we love to skirt the edges of propriety with winks, raised eyebrows and ambiguously provocative remarks. But it's a short step onto a very slippery slope, and a little sensual sparring can quickly spiral from cute and clever to distasteful and dangerous.

Watch your tongue. HBO and Showtime have made the worst kind of language positively pedestrian. But there used to be seven words you couldn't hear on television for good reason. Refinement of language reinforces refined behavior. Conversely, the more acceptable foul vocabulary becomes, the more likely we are to cross the boundaries of suggestive, harassing and bullying speech as well.

Look professional. The way you dress sends a signal about how you expect to be treated. The more casual the attire, the looser the standards. This applies to both productivity and personal interaction. A professional-looking workplace promotes professional behavior in every area.

Keep your hands to yourself. Aside from a formal handshake, touching has little place in any professional setting. Some people don't like being touched but are reluctant to say so. And unwanted or inappropriate contact is just another way of violating boundaries. Do you want people to think of you as "creepy"? Did you just find yourself thinking about Joe Biden?

Don't turn a blind eye. It's easy to convince yourself that a remark or action really meant nothing. You don't want to look petty, and you don't want to make something big out of something small. But if a colleague acts in a way that offends you, take that person aside and politely say you didn't appreciate it and please not to act that way again.

Have each other's backs. It's no different when you witness or learn of misbehavior toward others. It's hard for us to stand up for ourselves, especially when we aren't sure if we can count on those around us to come to our defense. Letting others know that you're there for them when they need you empowers everyone and creates a bulwark against predatory behavior.

Document. You can let a single, minor incident roll off your shoulders. But if it's egregious, or if a pattern of behavior begins to emerge, make sure to keep a detailed record in real time, in the form of personal emails, a personal diary and, if necessary, complaints to superiors.

Don't over-react. As diligent as we must be, we also have to be careful not to go overboard. Some speech is perfectly innocent, and an invitation to go out for dinner or a drink should not be interpreted as stalking.

In our politically correct society, too many people are eager to find misconduct everywhere, whether it's racial, sexual, or ideological. Occasionally, we all have poor judgment, and putting an offender on alert quietly and privately is probably enough for most first-offenses. Hitting the nuclear button at the slightest whiff of innuendo may end up being more harmful then helpful to a collaborative culture. If we're all walking on eggshells, none of us is going to get very far.

Don't believe it can't happen to you. The headlines and history are littered with stories of people who never thought they could become victims, never imagined they would become oppressors, or never believed they could be called out or brought down. When we think it *can't* happen to us, the chances rocket upward that it *will* happen to us.

King Solomon teaches that *wisdom walks in the ways of integrity and follows the paths of justice*. We can save ourselves from much folly by acknowledging the pitfalls that lie before us and disciplining ourselves to avoid them.

We take a critical first step by recognizing that all of us are capable of committing acts of gross impropriety, and that any of us can be tripped by the temptations of ego and opportunism if we let down our guard. Only when we hold ourselves to the highest standards of ethical conduct do we have the right to expect as much from others.

Practical Applications – *Dos* and *Don'ts*

- Do anticipate how benign behaviors might lead to destructive behaviors.
- Don't presume that good intentions will save you from poor judgment.

- Do take responsibility to stand up for yourself or others.
- Don't overreact and contribute to a culture of suspicion.

- Do exercise professional self-discipline in your speech and actions.
- Don't assume that others won't be bothered by comments just because you wouldn't be.

- Do conduct yourself at all times as if you were being recorded.
- Don't put yourself in situations that might turn out to be compromising.

- Do project professional courtesy at all times.
- Don't be afraid to ask if others are comfortable with situations as they are.

Step #12: *Be a model that inspires others*
Trait #12: *Pleasantness*

The verse in Leviticus clearly states that *you shall surely rebuke your neighbor*. Contemporary authorities, lamenting our collective inability to accept even the gentlest, most constructive criticism, warn against the likely fallout from offering unsolicited reproof.

Instead, they tell us that the most effective means of offering rebuke is to be a model of upright behavior yourself.

This works in two ways. First, if I want to be welcome in the company of quality people, I will hold myself to a higher standard of personal conduct so that I might be seen as worthy to share their space. The price of admission into the proximity of people possessing moral stature and pleasant demeanor is to cultivate my own refinement of character.

Second, in the same way that peer pressure can elicit coarse or thoughtless actions, so too can it motivate greater self-awareness and sensitivity. The more society as a whole projects an expectation of personal refinement and adherence to social niceties, the more uncomfortable it becomes for those who disregard the social contract, and the more they will be motivated to develop their own self-awareness and social self-discipline.

Seemingly trivial acts of making eye contact, smiling at strangers, uttering a greeting, and holding a door open – each of these helps bond society more tightly together while encouraging thoughtfulness and pleasantness from every quarter.

CHAPTER 13

Behind Window Number 2

Make more better choices

Why does Alaska have the highest rate of organ donation in the country? It might have something to do with former vice-presidential candidate Sarah Palin.

Most of us confront the question of whether or not we want our organs harvested every time we apply for a new driver's license. Typically, we have to choose between checking a box if we want to be donors or leaving the box empty if we don't.

This is how most donor forms were designed. Then researchers wondered what they could do to increase the number of participants. They came up with the bright idea of giving people a choice between two boxes: mark the *yes* box to donate, mark the *no* box to decline. Their reasoning went this way: if people can opt-out passively, they're not necessarily thinking about the choice in front of them; having to choose one way or the other forces them to consider their options more carefully, resulting in more affirmatives.

The reasoning makes perfect sense. However, people are not always reasonable.

That's what Judd Kessler of the Wharton School and Alvin Roth of Stanford discovered when they tested applicants in California and Massachusetts. Contrary to expectations, the open-ended option encouraged greater participation, whereas forcing people to choose *yes-or-no* made the number of donors drop.

The question, of course, is *why?*

Have you ever had the experience of someone telling you to do something you've already made up your mind that you want to do? If you're like most people, you probably decided in the next instant that you no longer wanted to do it.

The reason is obvious. Human beings are creatures of ego. We don't like to be *told*. We want to be in charge of our own decisions. The moment someone asserts command over us, our sense of independence pushes us in the other direction. This explains why manipulation through reverse psychology can be so effective (as long as it isn't recognized for what it is).

In the case of organ donation, the open-ended choice allowed people to feel that they were making a choice that was truly theirs. When forced to choose between alternatives, people may have felt pressured to participate and reflexively resisted by opting out.

So here's Takeaway #1. If you feel backed into a corner, your natural reaction will be to push back. But just because we're being pressured doesn't mean that the choice is a bad one. Surrendering before external pressure because we're weak or timid is no worse than digging in our heels because we're too stubborn to relinquish control.

Therefore, whenever you feel under pressure, take a step back and look at your options objectively. Try to separate the choice from the situation. By recognizing that emotions may be clouding your thinking, you have a better chance of neutralizing their influence over how you ultimately decide.

We can apply the same strategy when working with others as well. If you want to influence other people to make better choices, be a consultant: present the options with as little pressure as possible. As long as people *feel* in charge of their own decision-making process, they're less likely to circle the wagons to protect the status quo.

Doctor Kessler discovered something else as well. When subjects who had already made their choices one way or the other were later offered a chance to change their donor status, they were 22 times more likely to opt-in than to opt-out. Doctor Kessler believes that when we have to make decisions we haven't had time to think through, we're much more likely to err on the side of caution. But give us time to consider, and we're more likely to follow our hearts. No pun intended.

It's not surprising that more deliberation leads to more carefully thought-out decisions. But it does offer a further insight into the workings of the human ego.

Here's another experience you may have had. Remember our example of being deep in a heated debate, growing more passionate by the minute? Then, it suddenly dawns upon you that you're actually wrong and that your antagonist is right.

What do you do? Either a) immediately concede the point, or b) start arguing even more vociferously?

If you're like most people, you've gotten way too invested in your position to back down by admitting defeat. The realization that you've been wrong all along only prods you to save face by fighting harder to win.

It's okay to be wrong, okay to change your mind, okay to admit error. Much better, in fact, to acknowledge one's own mistake than to have someone else discover it and bring it to light.

But our willingness to concede error decreases in proportion to the intensity of our emotions. Conversely, the more comfortable we feel when considering the alternatives before us, the more likely we are to see different alternatives with equal clarity and objectivity. Even when that means we may have to admit we were wrong.

Which brings us to Takeaway #2. Avoid acting in the heat of the moment; take your time and keep cool. Let ideas percolate before putting them into practice, whether you're sending off emails, offering criticism to your spouse, or making career decisions. And all the more so when it comes to tattoos and casual dalliances. *Act in haste, repent at leisure* is a cliché for good reason.

So what does all this have to do with Sarah Palin?

Well, not that much, really. But it does have something to do with petroleum and drilling in the Alaskan wilderness.

The state of Alaska has vast territory, few people, and massive reserves of oil. Since 1976, every resident receives a cash dividend from state oil revenues which, in 2014, put $1884 in each person's pocket.

So when do you think the Alaska government asks people whether or not they want to be organ donors? That's right – in the same envelopes that contain their annual oil dividends.

Now ask yourself this: when would *you* be more likely to make some magnanimous gesture toward helping others – as you open up a check for a thousand dollars or after standing in line for half an hour and having to contend with governmental bureaucracy?

This makes Takeaway #3 a no-brainer. We all want to be good, want to be kind, want to be giving. We all want to the right thing and consider ourselves good people.

So when it comes to decision-making, we can do better by *creating* the circumstances that produce better decisions, both for ourselves and others

Want to sell your house? Make sure you have chocolate chip cookies baking in the over when prospective buyers show up at the door. Want to ask your boss for a raise? Try to time your request to coincide with his son making the dean's list or his daughter's engagement.

And what puts *you* in a good mood? Mellow music, inspirational stories, walks in the park, phone calls to the kids, a clever email, the company of friends... these are only an arm's reach away, and any one of them can instantaneously dispel frustration at work, stress over money, fear of national security threats, and disgust with politicians. Of course, we should listen to the news enough to know what's going on, but too much involvement in the problems of the world is poison to the soul.

But we can do even more than that. In a brilliantly entertaining and informative Ted Talk, psychologist Shawn Achor outlines a simple formula for reprogramming our brains to become more optimistic and generally positive:

Gratitude. Research shows that writing down three new reasons for being grateful every day for three weeks rewires the brain to see the world through a brighter lens.

Journaling. Writing about one positive experience in the last 24 hours allows your brain to re-experience the event. Instead of adding layers of bitterness by reliving unpleasant incidents, we can add sweetness to our lives by revisiting the good things that happen to us.

Exercise. Taking care of our bodies makes us more disciplined and reinforces our awareness that behavior matters. **Meditation.** Focusing on single, simple thoughts is the best antidote to our overloaded, over-scheduled, over-stimulated lives. **Random Acts of Kindness.** Something as small as sending an appreciative email once a day can reframe our outlook and extend feelings of positivity to others.

Instead of looking for things to make us happy, we need to recognize happiness as a state of mind we create for ourselves. When we do, we will make better decisions, enjoy greater success, and bring greater joy to the people around us and to the world.

A note of full disclosure: the author does not participate in organ donation for religious reasons, but has the greatest respect and admiration for those who do.

Practical Applications – *Dos* and *Don'ts*

- Do give others open-ended choices.
- Don't box others, or yourself, into binary options.

- Do be a consultant.
- Don't be drill sergeant.

- Do create associations between good outcomes and good choices.
- Don't compound your error by refusing to admit you're wrong.

- Do work to create an environment in which people want to make good choices.
- Don't dwell on negative thoughts that color everything around you in a negative light.

- Do develop the disciplines that will reprogram your brain for a better outlook.
- Don't tell yourself that you don't need fixes or that you can start tomorrow.

Step #13: Start all over again
Trait #13: Thrift

The sages teach that no one dies with even half his desires fulfilled. It is part of the human condition that no matter how much we have, we always want more.

This is why spouses cheat, why the wealthy steal, why the powerful risk everything trying to acquire more power. It is also why the sages taught, *Don't trust yourself until the day you die.*

Jewish tradition records the practice of Rabbi Eliezer who, despite being so rich that he owned whole cities of industry and fleets of merchant ships, nevertheless traveled from town to town carrying a bag of flour over his shoulder from which he kneaded and baked his own bread.

Rabbi Eliezer recognized the dangers of wealth, and therefore compensated by practicing extreme austerity to retain his perspective. By distancing himself from creature comfort and the honors others would have accorded him, he reminded himself that the true measure of a person is not what he has, but what he is and what he does.

The truth is, we *should* feel dissatisfied – not with our material wealth, but with the richness of our moral and spiritual accomplishments and stature. That's why the 13th step on the road to ethical recovery is to go back to the beginning, to start over with the sense of urgency of a poor person seeking his next morsel of bread.

Someone once said that the definition of a good person is one who is trying to be a better person. We can always do better, and we should never stop trying to better ourselves.

EPILOGUE

Action Plans

What now?

Ideas are like fireworks. They light us up, look pretty, and make us go, "Wow!" Then they disappear and leave us with the sad feeling that we should have done something more with them.

We need inspiration. We need vision. But we also need a plan of action. If we want to change our culture, we have to start by changing ourselves. And if we want to change ourselves, we need concrete steps to lead us in the direction we know we should be going.

In this section, we'll revisit each chapter and focus in on real-world action points that you can begin to put into practice today... and not later than tomorrow.

Start with *one* action point. Just one. Act on it at least once today, then twice tomorrow, three times the next day, etc. Do it more if you can. After one week, it should have started to become second nature.

Then go on to the next action point. But don't forget about the first. Ideally, keep a journal to record each incident, as well as any positive results you see. Keep track of your progress, and reflect at least once a month to make sure you're keeping at it.

These action points follow the chapters, but they are in no particular order. Start with the ones that are easiest so you can feel a sense of success. After a while, look for the ones in areas where you need the most improvement. The more consistently you apply them, the more success you will see. The more success you see, the more motivated you will be to continue.

And when the people around you start to comment on the changes, give them a copy of the book and encourage them to join you on your crusade to repair every broken window.

Chapter 1: Make better choices

- Reject the assumption that more choices are better.
- Recognize a choice between trivialities for what it is and discard it.
- Whenever possible, empower others by letting them choose.
- Resist being pushed into making choices when you need more time or information.
- Be alert for false comparisons.

*Cultivate **humility** by reflecting on the ethical process you use to make your choices, rather than on the outcomes you hope your choices will produce.*

Chapter 2: The better you look, the better you'll be

- Visualize yourself succeeding, not having succeeded.
- Choose professional attire that projects professionalism.

- Ask yourself if your speech and actions project quality and trustworthiness.
- Seek out friends and company who hold you to a higher standard of personal conduct.
- Be casual away from work to highlight the contrast at work.

*Acquire **peace of mind** by acknowledging responsibility to live up to the standards befitting a power greater than yourself.*

Chapter 3: How to make the ordinary extraordinary

- Express gratitude daily for things easily taken for granted.
- Find value in routine so it doesn't become rote.
- Resist the impulse to live in the future and in your imagination.
- Don't romanticize what you don't have.
- Recognize the purpose in what you're doing... or find something else to do.

*Generate **enthusiasm** by directing your energy and efforts toward the fulfillment of a higher purpose.*

Chapter 4: Is there always safety in numbers?

- Seek out dissenting voices.
- Encourage discussion and debate.
- Ask questions, even when you think you know the answers.
- Be extremely wary when everyone is in agreement.
- Create real "safe spaces" where all ideas and opinions can be evaluated honestly and respectfully.

Become more sensitive to **truthfulness** *through thoughtful reflection and by articulating your errors.*

Chapter 5: How ants survive rush hour

- Find a reason to compliment someone – and mean it!
- Find a reason to thank someone.
- When you catch someone making an inconsequential mistake, resist the impulse to point it out.
- When you feel you've done enough, do something more.
- Do something that provides benefit to others; then keep it to yourself.

Establish **order** *in your life by honestly and courageously identifying and prioritizing which of your character traits need refinement.*

Chapter 6: Make technology your servant

- Silence your phone in meetings.
- Turn your phone off when you're with people.
- Acknowledge calls and emails within 24 hours... ideally within two.
- Take a walk without your phone.
- Take a technology Sabbath – one day a week with no devices.

Develop **diligence** *by recognizing your place in the larger community and using all the resources available to become your best self.*

Chapter 7: Reclaiming Civility

- Allow others to explain themselves, then carefully consider their arguments and positions.
- Find a point worthy of agreement, then question whether there may be another way of looking at the issue.
- Address weak logic or dubious facts by questioning yourself first and asking for clarification: "I'm not sure I understand how that is so."
- Respond to attacks on your ideas without defensiveness by citing evidence to defend your position.
- Firmly stand your ground with being aggressive; remain calm and reasonable when others grow heated or irrational.

Practice **silence** in order to hear what others say so you can understand their points-of-view and thereby better evaluate your own.

Chapter 8: When in doubt – just ask!

- Find a reason to ask for someone's help; look for an opportunity to ask if someone needs your help.
- Make eye contact, say hello, and smile.
- Invite someone to participate in a project.
- Approach someone in a position of power or influence and ask their advice.
- Strike up a conversation with a stranger without ulterior motive.

*Demonstrate **respect** and earn trust by articulating back to others their ideas and positions so they know they have been heard.*

Chapter 9: Three tips for programming your moral GPS

- Ask yourself where your moral values came from.
- Read a short essay or book on classical morality and ethics.
- Try to explain to yourself why others might rationally hold opinions different from yours.
- Question your own motives and objectivity.
- Question the majority, especially when you're part of it.

*Become a defender of **justice** by confronting your own personal bias and emotion in order to protect yourself from indulging unreasonable attitudes and reaching unjustified conclusions.*

Chapter 10: Staying honest in a dishonest world

- Choose carefully the company you keep.
- Stick to the facts without embellishing or exaggerating.
- Be civil and courteous at all times, but call things what they are.
- Be skeptical of unverified information, admit error, and acknowledge truth.
- Look for the good in all things as much as possible.

*Maintain moral **cleanliness** by rejecting double standards and intellectual inconsistency, applying the same logic and rationale regardless of ideology or political considerations.*

Chapter 11: Post-victory let-downs are for the birds

- See every success as the starting point for the next goal.
- Find value and reward in every small victory.
- Remind yourself that working toward your goal is more rewarding than reaching it.
- Embrace short-term failures as opportunities.
- Don't ever begin a sentence with the phrase, "I'll be happy when..."

Increase **patience** *through meditation, acquiring greater self-awareness and respect for truth, thereby enjoying the benefits of wisdom in every aspect of your life.*

Chapter 12: Ten tips for a safer, healthier workplace

- Be aware of how things might look from the perspective of others.
- Anticipate where things might lead, even if you have no expectation of them leading there.
- Stand up for yourself and others when lines are crossed.
- Don't overreact to what might simply be social awkwardness.
- Make sure that your own conduct is a positive model for others.

Conduct yourself at all times with **pleasantness** *so that you become a model of refinement and character to inspire others.*

Chapter 13: Make more better choices

- Don't reduce all decisions to binary options.
- Think in open-ended terms, and present others with open-ended choices.
- Be generally positive and create a positive environment that promotes better decision-making.
- Help others clarify the options before them and likely consequences.
- Be self-disciplined in developing habits that rewire the brain for success and happiness.

*Adopt an attitude of **thrift**, taking pleasure in having less clutter and distraction in your life while seeing every milestone as an opportunity for new beginnings rather than a mark of completion.*

AFTERTHOUGHTS

Weather or Not, Your Time has Come

Climate is what you expect; weather is what you get.
~Robert A. Heinlein

We've certainly gotten our share of weather this season. Blizzards in New England, ice storms in Florida, subzero temperatures in the Midwest, and devastating dry heat in California. Whatever we were expecting from winter, this was not it.

Of course, you can always find a silver lining if you look hard enough. As humorist Kin Hubbard wrote, *Don't knock the weather; nine-tenths of people couldn't start a conversation if it didn't change once in a while.*

It is remarkable how much we seem to delight in stating the obvious. Do we think that others won't notice Mother Nature's current disposition if we don't bring it to their attention?

But the weather teaches a deeper lesson in human psychology, one first observed by the sages of the Talmud some 2000 years ago:

Everything is in the hands of heaven except cold and heat.

At first glance, it appears that the author of this remark was playing with our minds. After all, is anything *less* in our control than the weather? To complicate matters, this comment seems to contradict the more famous talmudic dictum that,

Everything is in the hands of heaven except the fear of heaven.

The meaning of the second statement is easier to grasp. As much as we human beings like to think of ourselves as masters of our own fate, the truth is that we have no control whatsoever over what happens to us.

Of course, we can choose how we act. But where our actions will lead, where our choices will take us, and what twists of fate lie lurking around every corner – about those we have nothing to say at all.

Consider these ironic footnotes to history:

- The trendy, textured wallpaper invented in 1960 by Marc Chavannes and Al Fielding turned out to be a total failure. Well, not a *total* failure. Several years later it was put to good use. You know it as Bubble Wrap.

- In 1968, Spencer Silver tried and failed to develop a super-strong adhesive for 3M laboratories. Instead, he produced a stickum that easily peels right off. His failure gave us Post-it notes.

- Then there's the story of John DeLorean, the wunderkind who rose to become general manager of Chevrolet, only to leave General Motors and start his own car company. His sleek, gull-winged, stainless steel luxury car captured the world's imagination, and experts predicted boundless success. But production delays and a global recession drove his company into bankruptcy. DeLorean was arrested and charged with drug-trafficking, purportedly to raise the $17 million he needed to save his ailing company.

Sometimes we do everything right and fail; sometimes we do everything wrong and succeed. Ultimately, we have no more control over the outcome of our efforts than we have over the weather. What we do control, however, is how we respond to what happens to us.

When we forget where we left our keys, do we start snarling at the people around us? When we're late for an appointment, do we curse the red light that makes us later? When we get caught making a mistake, do we try to deflect responsibility by shifting blame onto others? When a project fails, do we make excuses, or do we try to learn how to turn the experience of failure into a formula for success?

It's the way we respond to situations of stress that reflects the quality of our character – this is what the sages call *fear of heaven*.

Don't we do a greater service to ourselves, as well as to the people around us, when we laugh at our own foolishness, admit our own mistakes, and quietly accept the inconveniences that fate scatters along our way? Don't we make it easier for others to look for the good and cope with the bad when we model keeping perspective and priorities where they should be? Don't we come out ahead in the end by challenging ourselves to do better than by cursing the randomness of misfortune?

We can't change the weather, but we can dress warmly against the cold and stay hydrated against the heat. That's plain common sense.

It's less common to remain even-tempered and upbeat in the face of life's bumps and bruises. But it makes just as much sense.

And it's entirely in our hands.

Take Pleasure in Taking the High Road

We all know that two wrongs don't make a right. But does one right cancel out one wrong?

There's a good chance you believe that it does. Research suggests that our brains are wired to think of a good deed as a kind of get-out-of-jail-free card.

Psychologists call it licensing. It works like this:

You come home from a hard workout at the gym and immediately sit down to a double-helping of ice cream with chocolate syrup and whipped cream. The virtuous behavior of exercising makes you feel better about yourself, which then gives you license to indulge the less virtuous behavior of overdosing on sugar. The responsible act of taking care of yourself makes it easier to rationalize letting yourself go.

But Aaron Garvey and Lisa Bolton of the University of Kentucky have discovered that it goes even further than that.

WE ARE WHAT WE THINK

In their research, they took two groups of volunteers and gave them cookies to eat. The cookies were identical for each group, but in one group they were labeled "healthy." After finishing their cookies, the subjects were given candy.

As the psychology of licensing would suggest, subjects who had eaten the "healthy" cookies ate more candy than the other group. But not for the reason we might have thought.

Garvey and Bolton measured not only the amount of candy eaten but also the amount of pleasure experienced from the candy. They found that the candy actually tasted better to the people who believed they had eaten healthy cookies.

Professor Garvey identified two implications from his research. First, if we do something virtuous before indulging in pleasure, we can actually make the experience of pleasure more pleasurable.

Second, if we reframe our attitude toward responsibilities and acts of virtue by thinking of them as commitments that we want to do rather than obligations that we have to do, we can make vices less attractive and protect ourselves from the damaging fallout of licensing.

THE MOST ENDURING PLEASURE

These two implications teach us an electrifying lesson in human free will. Through disciplined thinking, I can choose whether to make my self-indulgence more or less pleasurable. And that discipline takes the form of how motivated I am to choose virtue over vice.

In other words, do I want to trick my brain into getting more pleasure from healthy acts or from unhealthy acts? And if getting more psychological pleasure from virtue means that I'll become less interested in the physical pleasure of vice, why would I ever want to choose vice over virtue?

We know from experience that physical pleasure is nothing more than psychological junk food. Enjoyments of the flesh feel good in the heat of the moment, but they leave a pleasure vacuum the instant they're over. In contrast, emotional pleasures linger, and profound emotional satisfaction endures long after the source of pleasure has passed.

Most of all, the warm feelings we can get from family, community, and the sense of contribution to a higher purpose stay with us constantly. The less we distract ourselves with empty physical gratification, the more intense and continuous those emotional pleasures become.

King Solomon says, *One who loves pleasure will be a man of want, and one who loves wine and oil will never become rich.*

In a society that has increasingly debased the nobility of human emotion, people say that they love their cars, they love to sleep, they love to go to the beach, they love steak and wine. But if these are the objects of our love, what emotion is left for us to feel for our husbands and our wives, for our parents and our children, for the sources of inspiration that beckon us to moderate our lust and pursue loftier, more satisfying ideals?

The comics page can give us a chuckle, but it doesn't enrich our minds like a good story. A jingle on the radio might get stuck in our head, but it doesn't move the heart like a symphony. A passing flirtation may set us briefly a-tingle, but it is a sorry substitute for a lifetime of commitment.

Anything worthwhile requires investment and effort. Life is too short to squander it on fleeting pleasures when there is so much real joy for us to find.

The Real Rainbow Coalition

The story of a Great Flood can be found in virtually every human culture. However, the biblical record stands alone in its dramatic conclusion: as Noah emerges from the ark, the Almighty sets His rainbow in the heavens as a sign that never again will He visit the waters of devastation upon the earth.

Much has been made of the shape of the rainbow – an inverted bow to direct the arrows of divine wrath away from mankind. But is this a hopeful sign? Does it not imply that we are in fact deserving of destruction? Does it not contain a warning, that only because of God's promise to Noah are we spared the natural consequences of our own moral corruption?

And what do the colors and beauty of the rainbow signify? Is it not incongruous to invoke something so beautiful as a reminder that a 4000-year-old covenant is all that stands between us and annihilation?

WANTING IT BOTH WAYS AND NO WAYS

In the old Peanuts comic strip, Linus declares that, "I love humanity; it's people I can't stand."

It's no longer a joke. As human society grows ever more fractured, we see everyone else as either too traditional or too progressive, too dovish or too hawkish, too far left or too far right. Unity remains a dream we no longer believe in as we divide ourselves up into increasingly tribal enclaves.

Paradoxically, it is the strength of conviction that separates people from one another. Too many of us believe that our way is more "beautiful" than anyone else's way, that only we are the chosen standard-bearers, and that we alone speak Truth while all others are heretics or infidels.

Why do we find it so difficult to celebrate our — dare I use the word — diversity? We give lip service to the value of multiculturalism, recognizing that our differences can make us greater than the sum of our parts. But then we use distinctiveness as a wedge to set ourselves apart from others.

In modern society, diversity often becomes a club to bludgeon into submission all whose sense of traditional values or personal integrity compels them to reject the moral anarchy that defines our times. Intolerance masquerades as forbearance, proclaiming an open-mindedness that is reserved only for those who conform to ideologically acceptable standards of cultural elites.

THE CHALLENGE OF MORAL EQUILIBRIUM

It was the same kind of violent division that brought the devastation of the Flood upon mankind. In that benighted generation, the law of the jungle drove human beings to an unthinkable level of bestial corruption. Had the Almighty not brought the waters of destruction upon the earth, human beings would surely have destroyed themselves.

Back then, it was selfishness and greed that tore society apart. Today, it is ego and ideology.

True, it's not easy to achieve the delicate balance between acceptance on the one hand and conviction on the other. Tilting too far to one side catapults us toward moral dogmatism; tilting too far to the other sets our moral compass spinning in all directions.

So what is the solution?

The answer lies in seeing the rainbow as both beautiful and terrifying. It is a symbol of diversity and how much we can achieve by celebrating our differences; but simultaneously it is a reminder of how much destruction we can bring upon our world when differences become justification for divisiveness.

To truly love our fellow human beings we cannot retreat into ideological isolation. If we do, we succeed only in marginalizing others in our own minds. Ultimately, we must take great care to chart a course between the extremes of ideology and accommodation.

So reach out to connect with someone outside your own close, closed, comfortable group. Engage people who think differently, not to debate but to exchange ideas and seek understanding. Remember as well that the most exquisite flowers, the most dramatic seascapes, and the most inspiring mountain peaks are those that reflect all the colors of the rainbow.

Acknowledgments

In the later years of his life, J. D. Salinger closeted himself away and wrote for his own pleasure – freed by success, he said, from the corrupting influence of having to please an audience or readership.

For those of us who see writing as communication, however, it makes little sense to write in a vacuum. Diaries are for private reflection; insights and observations are most meaningful when shared with the world.

I'm most grateful, therefore, to the editors who have seen fit to publish my words so that others might read, debate and, I hope, find some measure of enlightenment and inspiration in them. Binyamin Jolkovsky, editor-in-chief of *Jewish World Review*, has always received my submissions with enthusiasm and appreciation. Erin Falconer at *Pick the Brain* as well has provided me with a valued forum for ideas, as have the editors at *Finerminds*.

As always, Syd Chase has invested his time and much red ink to help me weed out verbal overgrowth and achieve greater clarity of thinking and expression.

My thanks to Gila Jacobsen for her creative assistance with cover design, and to Ed Robinson and Aprille Trupiano for helping inspire this collection. Also to Shankar Vendantam and NPR for the show *Hidden Brain*, which provided the springboard for many discussions.

Of course, my wife, Sara Miriam, tolerates me secluding myself in my office day and night and is a continuous source of strength, as are those readers who take the time to comment so that I know my words are not falling entirely on deaf ears.

Finally, my gratitude to the One who endows Man with insight and articulation, for sustaining me and bringing me to this and every milestone.

About the Author

A rabbi walked into a bar (after hitchhiking cross-country and sailing up the eastern seaboard in a yacht seized by the Coast Guard for drug trafficking) to enjoy a private performance by a jazz band that cost him the price of a beer.

No, this isn't a joke. This is a life.

Rabbi Yonason Goldson has hitchhiked across the United States, circumnavigated the globe, seen the Taj Mahal, the pyramids of Giza, and the tea plantations of Sri Lanka. He's hiked to the bottom of the Grand Canyon and to the tops of the Sierra Nevada. He's jumped out of an airplane and undergone open-heart surgery (but not at the same time).

He's studied at the University of Edinburgh, taught school in Budapest, Hungary, and seen Richard III performed in Ashland, Oregon, and Stratford-on-Avon. He earned a degree in English Literature from the University of California, taught high school for 23 years, published four books, raised four children, and been married to the love of his life for 30 years.

His greatest joy is to share his own inspiration with others. Whatever his audience, he makes them laugh, makes them cry, makes them think and makes them wonder – all in the hope that he will leave them with a sense of their own untapped potential and a road-map to guide them forward along the pathways to success and happiness.

Visit yonasongoldson.com and learn more about the Keynote Speaker with 3000 years' experience.

Resources

Please visit Yonason Goldson's website for a wealth of articles, essays, videos, and interviews drawing ethical lessons and insights from headline news, historical events, and the world of science and nature:

yonasongoldson.com   ethicalimperatives.com
info@ethicalimperatives.com (314) 489-5380

KEYNOTES AND SEMINAR PROGRAMS

Main Keynote: The Power of Ethical Leadership
Creating a culture of engagement, loyalty, and prosperity by seeing ourselves as others see us

According to estimates, as much as **$550 billion in productivity is lost every year** in the United States because of employee disengagement and $359 billion due to workplace conflict.

Can you afford not to take action?

In any community — whether corporate, congregational, or civic — the secret of success lies in creating a culture of mutual commitment, cooperation, and trust. And it all depends on clear and honest communication — which starts when we recognize that others often see us very differently from how we see ourselves:

- Do we act appreciative or entitled?
- Do we offer counsel or belittlement?
- Do we inspire confidence or suspicion?

Awareness of how we come across to others allows us to forge healthy relationships, promote productive meetings, and transform a group of individuals into a cohesive team. This keynote will give you:

- Entertaining stories and real-world examples of ethical conflicts
- A guide to foster cooperative spirit when dealing with others
- A strategy for holding ourselves to a higher standard of personal responsibility

Why choose Yonason Goldson for your event? Because his presentation will leave you with:

- A road-map for enhancing engagement, loyalty, and productivity
- The skills to develop ethical speaking and thinking
- The motivation to apply the principles of ethical communication for personal and professional success

The Ethics of Cultural Diversity — *How diversity can bring us together and make us stronger*

Have you ever wondered why opposites attract? There's a reason why we dream of exotic places and find fascination in fantasy. But when the unknown gets too close for comfort, enchantment quickly turns into anxiety.

It doesn't have to be that way. The differences between us provide endless opportunities for collaboration and success. Explore how changing our mindset toward differences can change our fortunes and our future.

Fix Your Broken Windows — *Little tweaks that make big differences in personal and professional culture*

We all know that small problems eventually turn into large problems, that benign neglect is rarely benign, and that the more any behavior becomes part of a culture the harder it is to change, no matter how corrosive it may be.

But if little problems grow large, why can't little fixes turn the tide? Sometimes all we need is to be reminded to do the things we know we should be doing already. Practice becomes habit, and good habits are the harbinger of real positive change.

Ethical Leadership Summit

Now it's time to put the principles of this book into practice. No matter what your business, *your image **is** your brand image.*

Do you want to earn the respect, trust, and loyalty of customers and clients, of colleagues and employees? Do you want to benefit from creating a culture of integrity and success?

This book is just the beginning. Next comes a deep dive into the sea of practical wisdom that can guide you to implement the principles of ethics into your business culture and relationships.

You can do it on your own. Or, we can do it together. This 2 ½-day summit brings together like-minded visionaries eager to take the 12-step ethical recovery concepts and mold them into laser-focused strategies, while simultaneously forging a tactical alliance of partners eager to support one another in the weeks and months that follow.

Inspiration is wonderful. Ideas are exciting. But they're not enough. It's what you do with them that really matters. It's what kind of game plan you devise to create an engaged, passionate, and enthusiastic community built on a foundation of ethical awareness and defined by a culture of dedication to higher purpose.

Does this sound exciting? Are you ready to learn more? If so, let's have a conversation: info@ethicalimperatives.com

What does a culture of ethical affluence look like?

- Engaged, enthusiastic, loyal, and productive employees
- Higher employee retention
- Increased cooperation, collaboration, and creativity
- Improved brand reputation and recognition
- Fewer conflicts and compliance issues

Learn more in my ebook
The Secrets of Ethical Affluence

Identifying what's going wrong is often easier than it seems. Fixing it may not be much harder. But both involve a formula made from ingredients that are often in short supply.

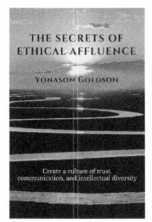

In the end, it all comes down to these CoDE of values: Communication, Diversity, and Ethics. Every successful enterprise is built on these three pillars. With them in place, the sky's the limit.

Request your free copy a
info@ethicalimperatives.com

ALSO BY YONASON GOLDSON

Proverbial Beauty
Secrets for success and happiness from the wisdom of the ages

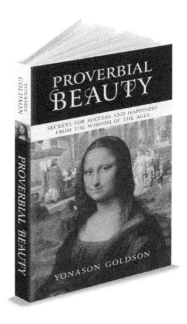

We live in a world of endless contradictions. Work vs. family. Money vs. fulfillment. Desires vs. obligations. The body vs. the spirit. We rely on conventional wisdom to point us forward. But conventional wisdom gets it wrong more often than we imagine.

Open this book and celebrate the marriage between the greatest collection of verbal images in history — King Solomon's *Book of Proverbs* — and the most famous visual image in the world — Leonardo Da Vinci's *Mona Lisa*.

- *Find tranquility in the midst of conflict*
- *Develop attitudes that deepen relationships*
- *Gain clarity through times of darkness and confusion*
- *Decrease cynicism and find joy in the daily miracles that fill our lives*

Take a guided tour beneath the surface of the world we live in through the lens of news stories, historical vignettes, folktales, the wonders of nature, and the discoveries of science — all woven together in a lyrical and surprising medley of the human experience.

Researchers have no explanation why people, when blindfolded, can't walk a straight line; but what is it about human nature that makes us wander in circles? What does former NYC Mayor Bloomberg's plan to ease Manhattan traffic with "congestion pricing" reveal about the way we make decisions? What can fig harvesting, migraine headaches, and two Miss America titleholders teach us about the underpinnings of emotional well-being?

The answers to 3000 years of questions are here, revealed for every seeker of truth and self-awareness in the language of our modern era. Guided by the wisdom of Solomon and the mysteries of the Mona Lisa, learn how to find tranquility in the midst of chaos, how to savor the moments of everyday life, and how to resolve the paradoxes of the human heart.

Testimonials

"We had the privilege of having Yonason Goldson present on ethics at our Winter Professional Development Conference. Rabbi Goldson was witty, entertaining, and thought-provoking. It was nice to have a different viewpoint on a topic that is critical, not just to our profession, but to our everyday lives."
   Chief Neal Rossow, retired
   Director of Professional Development, MI Police Chiefs Assn

"Yonason Goldson's presentation was exhilarating, stimulating, full of life and life's lessons, wonderful coping mechanisms, ethical, humorous and enlightened; he is a wonderful speaker, a joy to listen to."
   Lawrence M. Poger, CLU
   Life Member Million Dollar Round Table, St. Louis, Mo

"Rabbi Yonason Goldson presented 'Cultural Ethics' to a group of senior care industry professionals, ranging from social workers to business owners. The audience was engaged and entertained, while learning crucial information on acceptance and understanding. I have had several requests to invite him back for a presentation in the spring!"
   Lila Shepley, Certified Geriatric Care Manager
   A+ Aging Advantage, St. Louis

"You are a rock star."
   Elizabeth O'Keefe, CEO, Technical Productions, Inc.
   Professional Conference Management Association

"Here's the great piece: Yonason's presence did not teach; it actually modeled. We don't want a speaker to teach us something; we want him to have us think. And Yonason through his speech did just that. From the time he stepped on stage to the time he ended it, the audience was excited, engaged, and listening... which is really what his speech was about -- open-minded listening. Don't we all need that?"
Bob Kittridge, *Behavior Performance Consultant*
Kittridge Connection, Inc., Colorado Springs

"Most entertaining ethics presentation I've ever heard in 30 years."
CJ Gallihugh, *Behavioral Interventions, Inc.*
Indiana Association of Behavioral Consultants

Dear Rabbi Goldson:
WOW! Wonderful! So many gems of wisdom throughout - relevant for all times but seems especially pertinent in today's day and age!
Bob Burg, *Hall of Fame Speaker*
Coauthor of the best-selling Go-Giver series

Dear Rabbi Goldson,
"LOVED your talk. Wow, it is so captivating, interesting, thoughtful, and profound. Your message teaches us to be open to those who may not immediately look as if we will connect. Your scripting, delivery, and natural humor made this a rewarding and nurturing experience to listen to. Congratulations!!
Patricia Fripp, CSP, *Hall of Fame Speaker*
Past President, National Speakers Association

"THANK YOU! YOU'RE BRILLIANT; I appreciated your thoughtful, concise answers. I especially enjoyed the manner in which you delivered them. I was blown away by your ... closing statement/advice. Bravo!"

Crane Durham, Nationally Syndicated Radio Host

"I was fascinated by Yonason's background as a rabbi and a speaker, which led to an insightful conversation about the impact of ethics. He had a real impact on me. I immediately liked him. He has a very open way about him that draws you in and makes you want to learn more."

Dr. Diane Hamilton, CEO of Tonerra
Nationally syndicated radio host

"What a super cool guy!"

Mary Lou Kayser, Host, Play Your Position podcast

Dear Rabbi Goldson,
  "It is a great pleasure for me to congratulate you [on] your excellence as a speaker. You have a sense of humor that works well in engaging your audiences. I also admired the way in which you connected facts and concepts and used your mastery of the subject to field a good range of questions from the audience in a skillful way.
  "Personally, I greatly enjoyed working with you, and it would be a pleasure to do so again."

Peter H. Raven, President Emeritus
Missouri Botanical Garden, St. Louis, MO

Reviews and praise for
Proverbial Beauty

"The book is amazing, and I found myself taking notes before the first chapter even began. *This book is full of wisdom and is beautifully written in a way that makes it relatable to everyone. It took me awhile to read through because I was note-taking and such. It will be on my shelf and in my 'to read' pile for years to come!! Love it!"*
– Marisa Slusarcyk for Rogue-Reviews

"Real definitions of love and happiness are provided in a blend of proverbs and analysis that **will delight those thinkers who want a lively discourse** *of possibilities and alternative visions."*
– D. Donovan, Senior Book Reviewer for Midwest Book Review

"For readers who are looking for tranquility to savor their daily lives, **this book will give them the clarity to move forward.** *Emotional and spiritual maturity depend on how one looks at and how one handles daily life. There are many tips on how to handle life, despite the hardships, losses and disappointments, and always be smiling."*
– Mamta Madhavan for Readers' Favorite

Find it on Amazon.com now

Amazon Reader Reviews

Rabbi Goldson weaves together eloquent prose, delightful humor, and a humane outlook to create an easy-to-read but thought-provoking guide to making choices in life. What makes the book especially compelling is how he draws on such a variety of sources to illustrate his points: religious teachings, popular culture, scientific studies, and the etymologies and multiple meanings of words in the Hebrew language.

Thank you, Rabbi Goldson, for a great book. *Proverbial Beauty* provides so much practical wisdom that it should be read slowly with a pen to underline things. The book wonderfully brings lessons to life through ancient Jewish sources, stories, and The Mona Lisa. I was very impressed how Rabbi Goldson was able to weave all these sources into one book to provide lessons for self-improvement for every person.

WOW! Halfway through the introduction, I knew that I was already seeing the unveiling of wisdom

Commonly we see books and we are drawn by the cover or the name without really looking at the "guts" or the text. We assume. This is a book that should be handled differently, it's a book that brings awareness, helps to create self-awareness, become a stronger YOU.

I found *Proverbial Beauty* to be an amazing book that I could not put down! Yonason Goldson has shared his amazing insight regarding how to solve life's complicated issues simply by changing one's thoughts and attitudes and following the wisdom of our Biblical leaders and Sages.

He writes, "As we embark down the path of unanticipated danger, we may only discover much later how fortunate we were that obstacles appeared in our way to stop us in our course. The problems, frustrations, and inconveniences we curse when they arise often prove our greatest benefactors in the end." We need only to look into King Solomon's proverbs to find answers to today's problem.

This is not your average how-to book. It is a " MUST READ" if you are seeking to enjoy the fullness of what life has to offer.

The author of the book is an educator – teacher, lecturer, counselor. You would expect that the book is for a limited audience – religious Jews. Surprise is not even a word in this case. The book is to be read by a very wide audience. The book is about beauty – real and a counterfeit. It is a practical, user-friendly guide about life, complete with inspiring true stories and realistic examples.

The author combines broad erudition with deep and insightful understanding of our lives to give us effective tools to recognize beauty and reject forgery. This ability is of high importance in our, sometimes confusing, superficial but still beautiful world.

This book is filled with unique stories that illustrate how to live your life in a meaningful and happy way. It is so easy to become cynical in our world, but it's not the right way. *Proverbial Beauty* will brighten your outlook and broaden your view. The author clearly shows how conventional wisdom and groupthink lead people astray. I recommend this book wholeheartedly.

I've read many books about wisdom, insight, tranquility, and lots of other verbiage we tend to lump into "self-improvement." Some are good and some aren't. I always go into a book of this type wondering "will I get any meaningful take-a-ways" from this? or will it be just another feel good book that scratches the surface.

Proverbial Beauty was an excellent surprise as I read each passing page. Yonason Goldson does something that, quite honestly, I would have never believed. He utilized the wisdom of King Solomon's proverbs and the mysterious beauty of the Mona Lisa and melded them together into a melting pot of perfect wisdom. This doesn't happen all at once, it occurs step by step, page by page. I found myself truly understanding exactly what he's talking about. This is a great book for those wanting a good perspective on what wisdom is and how to obtain it.

Be careful. After reading the book your eyes might open wider and you can see beauty in the world that was previously hidden from you.

Goldson really tackles a piece that is missing from our puzzle today. We have plenty of information and we have a lot of quick thinking folks with the ability to memorize a lot of facts and recall them easily. The missing piece? Wisdom. Our 21st Century world is sorely lacking when it comes to wisdom and understanding... and Goldson does a wonderful job of showing how our world fails often for lack of wisdom and shows us how to begin finding wisdom. Wonderful anecdotes and parables from Rabbinic traditions. And, he weaves it all around the timeless beauty of the Mona Lisa. I highly recommend this reading to anyone who realizes that something is missing. Goldson points us in the right direction.

This book provides readers with ancedotes, stories and evidence that will help them to discover themselves and take a good hard long look at them and reflect on how they too can become a better person. This book unlike a lot of the New Age type self-help guides that I have read, I quite enjoyed as it includes the wise words of historical figures and evidential wisdom from people such as King Solomon whom we all knew as the Wise King from the Bible to Leonardo da Vinci who painted the Mona Lisa painting which adorns the front cover of the book to more modern day people like author Michael Crichton and Jewish Rabbi Akiva and President Richard Nixon. So readers, if you are finding your life a bit lacking in the wisdom department , then check out your copy of Proverbial Beauty which is aimed to set you on the right path and as you will discover as you open the pages and flip through the many chapters , that often what you view as conventional and everyday wisdom can often be the wrong way of being wise and that sometimes in order to find yourself and discover your own little pottle of wisdom - you have to think outside the box and be a tad unconventional and you will notice more people following your examples as it often takes just one person to change their ways and the rest will follow.

Thought provoking and timely in this day and age.

Is your life going the way it should? Read *Proverbial Beauty* and think about where your life is heading. Reassess your values and reset your clock. Proverbial Beauty is a reality check in beautiful prose interspersed with pertinent stories emphasize each message. Hey, there are things in this world that are more important than Facebook and Twitter. Rabbi Goldson will help you discover what King Solomon wanted you to know and what the Mona Lisa already knows.

Books that inspire one or another are far and few in between because they all come off the same... typical self-help guru nonsense. This book is different which is why I chose to give it a read, wouldn't you be wondering as I what makes this not just another self-guide book?

This book provides readers with anecdotes, stories and proof or evidence to support. What makes it even better is how the author is his approach. The author just doesn't slam you with a bunch of you should do this or that, or if you accomplished so and so task good job, he shows you that throughout history if it's through events of leadership, to art, artist, inventors etc. as we look through the stories, the anecdotes the author shows you in ways that as hard things are we are and have never been alone in what we are feeling as many before has gone through similar struggles, hardship and loss, as we know things are not just black and white and transparent there is always a grey areas...but does not mean we can't be the best version of ourselves or try.

It's a book worth reading. A book worth checking out. Cause in the end if it's in the work place, in our own personal relationships or how we handle or discuss things we may all need or not a little friendly nonjudgmental advice on how we can improve.

Made in the USA
Monee, IL
03 September 2022

12148534R00079